Training the Technical Work Force

Anthony P. Carnevale
Leila J. Gainer
Eric R. Schulz

Training the Technical Work Force

 Jossey-Bass Publishers

San Francisco   •   Oxford   •   1990

T
65
.C38
1990

TRAINING THE TECHNICAL WORK FORCE
by Anthony P. Carnevale, Leila J. Gainer, and Eric R. Schulz

Copyright © 1990 by: Jossey-Bass Inc., Publishers
350 Sansome Street
San Francisco, California 94104

Jossey-Bass Limited
Headington Hill Hall
Oxford OX3 0BW

American Society for Training and Development
1630 Duke Street, Box 1443
Alexandria, Virginia 22313

Library of Congress Cataloging-in-Publication Data

Carnevale, Anthony Patrick.
    Training the technical work force / Anthony P. Carnevale, Leila J.
Gainer, Eric R. Schulz.
        p.   cm. — (The Jossey-Bass management series)
    Includes bibliographical references.
    ISBN 1-55542-201-2 (alk. paper)
    1. Technical education.   2. Technicians in industry—Training of.
I. Gainer, Leila J.   II. Schulz, Eric R.   III. Title.   IV. Series.
T65.C38 1990
607'.1—dc20   89-48806
                                                                      CIP

Manufactured in the United States of America

JACKET DESIGN BY WILLI BAUM

FIRST EDITION

Code 9009

The Jossey-Bass Management Series

ASTD Best Practices Series:
Training for a Changing Work Force

The material in this project was prepared under Grant No. 99-6-0705-75-079-02 from the Employment and Training Administration, U.S. Department of Labor, under the authority of Title IV, part D, of the Job Training Partnership Act of 1982. Grantees undertaking such projects under government sponsorship are encouraged to express freely their professional judgment. Therefore, points of view or opinions stated in this document do not necessarily represent the official position or policy of the Department of Labor.

Contents

Preface

Technical workers represent about 18 percent of the American work force, and it is generally believed that they receive a significant share (roughly 30 percent) of the $210 billion that employers spend on training annually. Moreover, technical workers are known to be especially important to American competitiveness because they are the lifeblood of industries that produce the lion's share of internationally traded products and services. In addition, technical workers invent and produce technologies that result in the "upskilling" of all workers. The continuous integration of new technologies with more highly skilled labor is widely recognized by labor economists as the true source of American competitiveness.

Training the Technical Work Force provides an overview of technical training in the United States, including the size and scope of the technical work force, how these workers get their training and who provides it, and how training is structured inside employer institutions. The book examines the occupations defined as technical and the number of people working in those occupations in the United States; takes a look at where in an organization technical training is designed, developed, and delivered; and discusses the connection between technical training and the strategic goals of the organization. The book also aids employers and educators by discussing the entities outside employer organizations that deliver technical training. Examples and case studies are provided throughout to illustrate the many different structures and strategic connections described in the overview.

This book is the result of research underwritten by a grant from the U.S. Department of Labor (DOL) and conducted under the auspices of the American Society for Training and Development (ASTD), a nonprofit professional association representing approximately 50,000 practitioners, managers, administrators, educators, and researchers in the field of human resource development.

The information in this volume reflects only some of the findings gathered during a thirty-month research effort that explored training practices in America's employer institutions. Other findings are detailed in two companion books, *Workplace Basics: The Essential Skills Employers Want* and *Training in America: The Organization and Strategic Role of Training,* and a companion manual, *Workplace Basics Training Manual,* that provides a step-by-step process for establishing a basic skills program in the workplace (all published by Jossey-Bass). In addition, the project produced five booklets that were published in 1988 and 1989: *Workplace Basics: The Skills Employers Want, The Learning Enterprise, Training America, The Next Economy,* and *Training Partnerships: Linking Employers and Providers* (available from ASTD, 1630 Duke Street, Box 1443, Alexandria, Va. 22313).

How the Research Was Conducted

The ASTD-DOL project was staffed by a team of ten professionals and a support staff. This team was greatly assisted by ASTD members who volunteered their expertise and provided access to their own corporations. In addition, experts from the fields of economics, adult education, training, public policy, and strategic management contributed analyses that provided a contextual backdrop for our work.

In 1986, when we launched this project, we did so with a determination that we would conduct applied research. Throughout the project, we kept our sights firmly focused on the real world, exploring what makes the technical work force tick and the training that keeps it ticking. In all study areas, including technical training, we began by surveying the current literature, looking for trends and patterns; this effort helped us identify the leaders in various disciplines and draw some preliminary conclusions. We tested our preliminary findings on a cadre of individual experts drawn from ASTD's membership and asked those members to identify other experts and practitioners who might provide feedback and insights. We continued along this path, and our list of contacts grew. From them we formed advisory panels that met during 1987 to advise us on our direction and findings. We also built networks of more than 400 experts and practitioners (the technical network alone had 114 members) who received periodic updates of findings and were asked for feedback.

Corporations and other private and public employer institutions were tapped extensively to provide actual examples of successful training systems and practices. We conducted on-site studies and much telephone interviewing, using specially constructed interview instruments that ensured we would gather uniform information. These employer "snapshots" are used throughout this book to complement and illustrate our findings and support the theoretical underpinnings of our work.

In developing our first-draft reports, we enlisted more than thirty experts and practitioners to review and comment on them. Their insights are reflected in this book, which constitutes our final report.

Who Should Read This Book

The findings in *Training the Technical Work Force* are designed to provide readers with an understanding of America's technical work force, the learning systems that keep that work force well skilled, and how actual corporations are managing their technical training needs. We believe that it can serve as a useful reference document on technical training for many years to come. Its intended audience includes executives and managers in all kinds of public and private organizations that employ and/or train technical workers; human resource development and training practitioners; personnel and human resource management practitioners; business and management consultants; vocational educators; college and university administrators; and academics in the fields of education, business management, industrial relations, and other areas.

Organization and Content

Readers should view this book as a compendium of facts, figures, and case examples. It has six chapters.

Chapter One explores the definition of technical training and what constitutes technical training, the size and scope of the technical work force, how technical workers are prepared for their jobs (qualifying training), and how they keep their technical skills up-to-date (upgrading training).

Chapter Two examines how technical training is structured inside employer institutions. This chapter also provides an analysis of the systems that employers use to deliver technical training and how those systems are connected to strategic goals.

Chapter Three looks at the many providers of technical training from educational institutions to original equipment manufacturers through vendors. It also explores how employers and providers share information and views about technological trends and future training needs, and forge partnerships to develop and deliver training programs.

Chapters Four, Five, and Six contain examples of how some of the nation's largest employers organize and deliver technical training to their work force.

Acknowledgments

Special thanks to Shari L. Holland, who served as research assistant on the project; Dawn Temple, Kim Genevro, and Stacey Wagner, who provided administrative assistance; Diane L. Charles, who managed our research symposium and the production of the manuscript; Diane Kirrane, who provided editorial assistance; and Gerald Gundersen and Ray Uhalde of the U.S. Department of Labor, who provided insights and guidance along the way.

The project team also wishes to acknowledge the contributions of the following experts, who consulted with us and provided contextual analyses: Eileen West and Rick West of West Training and Logistics Systems, who also provided some of the corporate examples; Harold Goldstein, former commissioner of the U.S. Bureau of Labor Statistics; Robert Craig, former vice president (ret.) of ASTD; William Ashley and Roy Butler of the National Center for Research in Vocational Education, Ohio State University; Joe Bieddenbach of the University of South Carolina's Swearingen Engineering Center; and Richard Clapper of the National Aeronautics and Space Administration.

Finally, we want to thank our advisory panel and network participants, who contributed their advice and counsel.

Alexandria, Virginia   Anthony P. Carnevale
February 1990   Leila J. Gainer
             Eric R. Schulz

The Authors

Anthony P. Carnevale was project director and principal investigator for the ASTD-DOL project and is chief economist and vice-president of national affairs for ASTD. Carnevale also currently serves as a board member of the National Center on Education and Employment at Columbia University; the National Center on Education and the Economy, cochaired by Mario Cuomo and John Scully; and the National Commission on the Skills of the American Work Force, comprised of America's leading business executives, union leaders, education and government officials.

Prior to joining ASTD, Carnevale was the government affairs director for the American Federation of State, County, and Municipal Employees (AFSCME). He also served as a comoderator for the White House Conference on Productivity and as chairman of the Fiscal Policy Task Force for the U.S. Council on Competitiveness. Carnevale has held positions as senior policy analyst for the U.S. Department of Health, Education, and Welfare; senior staff economist for the U.S. House of Representatives Government Operations Committee; and senior staff member for education, employment, training, and social services for the U.S. Senate Committee on the Budget. He also was a high school teacher and social worker in his home state of Maine. Carnevale was coauthor of the principal affidavit in *Rodriguez* v. *San Antonio,* a U.S. Supreme Court action to remedy unequal tax burdens and education benefits.

Carnevale has a Ph.D. degree from the Maxwell School of Public Affairs, Syracuse University. He holds M.A. degrees in social science and in public administration from Syracuse University and a B.A. degree in intellectual and cultural history from Colby College.

Leila J. Gainer managed the daily operations of the ASTD-DOL project and is ASTD's director of national affairs. She serves as a member of the advisory board for the Center for Business and Government Services of the Northern Virginia Community College and as a member of the National Alliance of Business advisory committee on structural work-based learning. In 1989 she also served as an informal adviser to ABC and PBS for the Project Literacy U.S. (PLUS) Campaign.

Before joining ASTD, Gainer directed the Center for Regional Action for the National Association of Regional Councils (NARC), working with state and local government-elected officials around the nation. In her nine years at NARC, Gainer served as director of federal liaison, communications and research; Washington information coordinator; and editor of the *Washington Report*. While at NARC, Gainer was honored by President Carter for her efforts leading to passage of the Rural Development Act of 1980. Gainer served as a reporter and editor for Commerce Clearing House, Inc.'s (CCH) bi-weekly publications *College and University Report* and *Commodity Futures*. In the early 1970s she was managing editor of CCH's *Labor Law Guide* and on the staff of *Labor Law Report*. Gainer has a B.A. degree from Frostburg State College, Maryland.

Eric R. Schulz was the researcher for the technical training and measurement portions of the ASTD-DOL project. Before joining the project, Schulz was a human resource research associate with Honeywell. He is a graduate of the University of Louisville and holds an M.A. degree in industrial relations from the University of Minnesota.

Technical Training Advisory Panel

Ted Allison
Director of Human Resource
Support Systems
McDonnell Douglas Astronautics
Company

Rod Boyes
Vice President
GMI Engineering and Management
Institute

Ralph Dosher
Corporate Manager
Education, Training, and
Development
Texas Instruments, Inc.

Gerald Gundersen
Chief, Research
United States Department of
Labor

Robert Hofstader
Manager
Education and Development
Exxon Central Services

Charlie Hoover
Chairman
Research and Development
American Telephone & Telegraph

Nancy Kuhn
Manager
Education and Training
Aluminum Company of America

Mike Liptrot
Manager
Training Development and
Employee Relations
Morton Thiokol, Inc.

John Robinson
Manager
University and External Relations
Motorola Training and
Education Center

Richard T. Sands
Senior Trainer
Merck Sharp & Dohme

Julie Walter
Manager of Training
Crouse-Hinds/Cooper
Industries

Harold Goldstein
Advisor
Technical Training

Eileen West
Advisor
Technical Training

Technical Training Network

Ted Allison
McDonnell Douglas
Astronautics Company

Steven Austin
FMC Corporation

G. E. Baker
Texas A&M University

Douglas J. Barney
Northern Telecom, Inc.

John P. Bartoszek
Ayerst Laboratories

Nancy Bauder
Bell Atlantic System Leasing

William C. Bean
International Business Machines

Joseph Benkowski
Miller Brewing Company

Rick Bilbro
Carolina Power & Light Company

Herman Birnbrauer
Institute for Business and Industry

Ambrose Bittner
United States Department of Labor

Rod Boyes
GMI Engineering and Management
    Institute

Franklin Brown
Horizon's Technology, Inc.

Elizabeth J. Carlisle
Ticor Title Insurance

Christina Caron
British Embassy

Patrick A. Cataldo
Digital Equipment Corporation

M. Linda Chapman
Washington State Department of
    Personnel/Employee Development
    and Training Division

Ivan Charner
National Institute for Work and
    Learning

Vernon C. Dahlstrom
TRW — Ross Gear Division

Thomas R. Denman
Fischback & Moore Incorporated

Robert DeSio
National Technological University

David P. Desrosier
Harris Corporation

Robert Deitrich
Kroger Company

Ralph T. Dosher, Jr.
Texas Instruments, Inc.

Kent Dubbe
Minnesota Mining and
    Manufacturing Company

Philip S. Edwards
WE Partners Company

Michael Emmott
Manpower Service Commission

Charles Fields
Hartford Steam Boiler and
    Insurance

Gene Freid
Agway, Inc.

Frank Furey
Polaroid Corporation

Lane R. Garrison
Sierra Pacific Power Company

Clyde W. Gast
Weirton Steel Corporation

Norman J. Goc
International Business Machines

Irvin Gordon
Independence Bancorp

Eric Frank Grosse
United Telephone Company of Ohio

Charles B. Gustafson
Technical Instructional Institute

Robert L. Halik
Allied-Signal EMS Sector

Kent W. Hamlin
Institute of Nuclear Power
    Operations

Marlys Hanson
Hanson & Associates

William M. Harral
ARCH Associates

G. Richard Hartshorn
Ford Motor Company

Larry Hirschhorn
Wharton Center for Applied
Research

Ross L. Hodgkinson
TACK

Robert A. Hofstader
Exxon Central Services

Richard D. Holzrichter
Panhandle Eastern Pipeline
Company

Charlie Hoover
American Telephone and Telegraph

Angie Howard
INPO

William Jenkins
Power Safety International, Inc.

Marilyn Joyce
The Joyce Institute

Chip Kehoe
Perkin-Elmer

Thomas J. Kruse
Reynolds Aluminum International

Nancy Kuhn
Aluminum Company of America

Larry E. LaForce
Harris Corporation

Robert J. Lanphear
Westinghouse Materials of Ohio

Don Ledbetter
Loral Data Systems

David LeSage
NASA

Bernard Libertore
Diebold, Incorporated

Michael S. Liptrot
Morton Thiokol, Inc.

Harry Litchfield
Deere and Company

Gale Long
Omark Industries

Nicholas P. Luzak
Philadelphia Electric Company

William Mallory
Ford Motor Company

Margaret L. Maloney
Goldome Realty Credit Corporation

Paul Manning
INPO

Barry J. Martin
Cardinal Industries, Inc.

Michael Mead
Chemlawn

James Meadows
Tampa Electric

Larry G. Meese
Northern Telecom

Celeste Miller
CAM Writers

Robert L. Morris
Boston Edison Company

Roy W. Murphy
Rohm & Haas Delaware Valley

Theodore Nagy
Borg Warner Corporation

Thierry Noyelle
Conservation of Human Resources

Jay Orlin
Northern Telecom Semi-Conductors
Group

Philip J. Papola
Consolidated Edison

Phil Parizino
Deluxe Check Printers

Michael R. Pellet
M-Squared, Limited

Training the
Technical Work Force

CHAPTER 1

The Special Role of Technical Workers and Technical Training

Technology will continue along its evolutionary path into the 1990s and beyond, bringing new challenges for those who toil on the production line, in the laboratory, and in the office. Computerization, robotics, and other sophisticated automation hold the promise of new opportunities for efficiencies and innovations. But to seize these opportunities—and to surmount the challenges that are to come—the United States needs a well-trained technical work force.

Most employers agree that this nation's future prosperity depends on the energy, flexibility, and creativity of a well-trained work force that is knowledgeable, innovative, efficient, and dedicated to quality (William T. Grant Foundation Commission on Work, Family, and Citizenship, 1988). Increasingly, however, these same employers are concerned that securing the quality and quantity of technical training required to build such a work force is the greatest challenge of all.

For employers that utilize technical workers, the skills of America's emerging labor pool (ages sixteen to twenty-four) and the demands of more and more sophisticated technologies are on a collision course. It is ironic that as the workplace becomes more technologically complex, the rising pool of available workers is lacking in many of the simplest and most basic skills, including reading, problem solving, computation, and knowing

1

how to learn. In fact, fully 30 percent of those potential workers are likely to come from populations that are disadvantaged — the poor, unemployed, or unemployable (Butler, 1988).

Moreover, technical work requires more education and training than any other work. Training in a technical discipline must be preceded by a sound grounding in the *basic* skills that prepare an individual to understand and acquire the more sophisticated constructs of technical work. This places a premium on the individual who has the basics and is therefore equipped to handle higher-level technical training. Given the demographic picture, building tomorrow's technical worker may very well mean doing so from the basics up — a costly and time consuming endeavor.

What is Technical Training?

Technical workers are people who use principles from the mathematical, physical, or natural sciences in their work. For the most part, they are employed in industries that rely on the application of scientific and mathematical principles to create products, services, or processes. To perform technical work, employees need a theoretical understanding of their jobs and the physical capability to accomplish the tasks of those jobs according to established performance standards.

Technical training enables individuals to apply theories and principles of natural and physical science to technical problems. It imparts an understanding of the scientific or mathematical base underlying the performance of a task. And it illustrates the physical aspects of the technical task. This blending of scientific and mathematical knowledge with actual performance qualifies training as technical. For the purposes of this book, technical training does not apply to disciplines such as law, the humanities, or the social sciences, in which scientific or mathematical theory is not required.

Mapping Technical Training:
The Size and Scope of the Technical Work Force

Attempts to define technical training and the technical work force are always somewhat arbitrary. The definition used here — that technical employees use theoretical principles from mathematics or the natural sciences in their work — is no exception. In general, this definition includes technical professionals such as scientists, doctors, and engineers; technicians such as dental hygienists, drafters, and broadcast technicians; and skilled trade (blue-collar) workers such as those in construction and manufacturing. A list of occupations requiring technical training appears in the appendix.

By this definition, there were 20.3 million technical workers in the United States in 1986, representing 18.2 percent of the American work force. Technical professionals made up 24 percent of the technical work force, technicians made up 18 percent, and skilled trade workers made up 58 percent.

In addition to technical employees, there are two related categories of workers. The first includes technical support employees, such as technical managers and sales and marketing personnel. These people work in institutions whose products or services are technically based. People in technical support jobs require some technical knowledge and often already have a technical background. The second related category is composed of technical education and training personnel — the teachers, professors, and trainers who prepare the technical work force.

Table 1 compares the training and development of technical employees with all other types of employees. It shows that the nation's 4.8 million technical professionals get the most education and training in preparing for their jobs and the most upgrading once on the job. Principal among technical professionals are the nation's 2.5 million health professionals, 1.5 million engineers, and 800,000 natural, mathematical, biological, and computer scientists. The 3.5 million technicians get more education and training in preparation for their jobs and upgrading once they are on the job than any other occupational group except technical and nontechnical professionals. More than 1.5 million technicians are in the health field, including nurses, physical therapists, X-ray technicians, and other operators of diagnostic equipment. Almost 1.3 million technicians such as circuit board assemblers and quality control technicians who oversee laser equipment in automobile assembly plants are in

Table 1. Sources of Qualifying and Upgrading Training: All Employees.

Occupational Group	Percentage with Qualifying Training				Percentage with Upgrading			
	Total	From School	Employer-Based Formal	Employer-Based Informal	Total	From School	Employer-Based Formal	Employer-Based Informal
All employees	55	29	10	26	35	12	11	14
Nontechnical professionals	92	87	6	16	47	47	10	11
Management support specialists	77	52	11	38	52	20	20	17
General managers	71	43	12	39	47	18	17	16
Clerical	57	33	7	31	32	10	10	15
Sales	43	15	12	28	32	7	13	15
Service	36	13	9	18	25	7	8	12
Transportation	36	2	8	26	18	2	6	9
Machine operators	37	6	6	26	22	3	4	16
Laborers	18	2	2	13	14	2	2	10
Technical professionals	94	83	14	23	63	25	23	17
Technicians	85	58	14	32	52	20	18	19
Craft	66	11	16	44	26	7	7	13
Precision production	61	17	15	38	36	8	13	18
Mechanics and repairers	68	19	18	39	44	7	22	17
Extractive	56	4	13	48	34	6	13	18

Source: Carey, 1985.
Note: Individual percentages can add up to more than the totals because some employees received training from more than one kind of source.

engineering and the sciences. Another 800,000 are broadcast, computer, and air traffic technicians.

There are almost 11.8 million skilled trade workers, including those in precision production jobs: mechanics, installers, repairers, and extractive (mining) workers. These workers receive only slightly more education and training to qualify for their jobs and upgrading once they are on the job than does the average worker. Moreover, they rely much more heavily on informal learning for preparation and upgrading than do technical workers.

Not included in the 11.8 million estimate are the nation's machine operators and assembly workers, although their jobs are increasingly technical in content. Automated manufacturing is increasing the depth and range of skills required in its jobs. As a result, many of the 7.6 million machine operator and assembly jobs are being reconfigured into fewer jobs that combine higher skill requirements and more technology; they are, in effect, being upgraded into technical jobs. Although the size of the technical work force is difficult to quantify, many operator and assembly workers clearly have already become technical workers, including as many as 2 million operators and assemblers who work in high-tech industries. Table 1 reveals that these workers receive less qualifying training than craft workers receive and little training once they are on the job.

The distribution of technical workers is uneven throughout the economy, with the largest number located in the service sector, principally in health care. Manufacturing employs about 14 percent of all technical workers.

The construction industry has the highest concentration of technical workers (33 percent of all construction workers are technical workers). The mining, transportation, and utilities industries are next, with nearly 20 percent of their employees in technical occupations. Of the employees in manufacturing, services, and government, about 16.7 percent (one worker in six) are technical workers.

Although the workers in some technical occupations such as health care are predominantly women, men generally dominate the technical work force, representing 76 percent of all technical workers. Table 2 shows that women, blacks, and Hispanics are generally underrepresented in the technical work force.

Table 2. Employment in Technical Occupations
by Sex, Race, and Ethnicity, 1986.

	Women	Blacks	Hispanics
All workers	44.4%	9.9%	6.6%
Technical workers	24.3	6.4	4.8

Source: Goldstein, 1988.

About 1.5 million technical workers are self-employed, principally as doctors, engineers, carpenters, mechanics, and repair workers.

As shown in Table 3, technical workers earn well above the average for all workers. Male technical workers earn more than their female colleagues, but the disparity is less in technical occupations than in the economy as a whole. Female technical workers earn 84 percent of what male technical workers earn, whereas in the economy as a whole, female earnings are only 69 percent of male earnings.

Table 3. Median Weekly Earnings, 1986.

	Both Sexes	Men	Women	Ratio
All workers	$358	$419	$290	.69
Technical workers	$482	$501	$420	.84

Source: Goldstein, 1988.

Training and Educating the Technical Work Force

Technical Professionals. Technical professionals are educated and trained to make broad judgments, to invent, and to apply a particular intellectual discipline to problem solving. They are responsible for developing new products and designs, enhancing existing products, and conducting research. Those involved in health care are responsible for diagnosing illnesses and prescribing treatment. Some may be responsible for formal management or exercising direct authority over subordinates.

Technical professionals are among the most highly educated and best trained of the nation's employees (see Table 4). Relative to other employees, they tend to receive very substantial amounts of formal education and employer-provided formal and informal training in qualifying for their jobs and upgrading their skills once they are on the job.

All technical professionals rely heavily on schools to prepare them for their jobs, although relative to other technical professionals, engineers and mathematical and computer scientists rely less on schools and more on employers for the training they need to qualify for their jobs. This suggests that engineering, mathematical, and computer jobs are more tailored to a particular industry and product. Engineers, as well as natural and computer scientists, rely on formal employer training to a greater extent than schooling for their upgrading.

Health care professionals receive the most upgrading, relying upon schools more than their employers for both qualifying and upgrading training. This suggests that their skill needs are not particularly employer-specific and that a stronger bond exists between health care professionals and their professional specialty than between the professional and a specific employer.

Recognizing the high degree of individualized training required to keep the technical professional up-to-date in his or her discipline, companies have traditionally played a relatively passive role in training their technical professionals. The company role has most often been one that focuses on underwriting the cost of training, advising workers on course selection, and delivering training that could be considered generic (technical training that addresses new technologics and processes introduced on the job, explains new applications of existing technology, or demonstrates new products). In recent years, however, competitive pressures have forced companies to integrate the development and design of innovations with production and marketing. This attempt to build more integrated structures is leading employers to play a more active role in the development and delivery of training and human resource development for their technical professionals.

Nevertheless, professional development for technical professionals remains a largely autonomous activity. While most

Table 4. Sources of Qualifying and Upgrading Training: Technical Professionals.

Occupational Group	Percentage with Qualifying Training				Percentage with Upgrading Training			
		From School	Employer-Based			From School	Employer-Based	
	Total		Formal	Informal	Total		Formal	Informal
Architects	94	91	13	31	41	10	7	23
Engineers	90	73	14	33	57	23	28	18
Health care professionals	96	96	10	7	72	33	8	8
Mathematical and computer scientists	90	66	26	41	65	21	36	24
Natural scientists	97	91	9	26	59	30	25	15

Source: Carey, 1985.
Note: Individual percentages can add up to more than the totals because some employees received training from more than one kind of source.

training for technical professionals is intended to update skills or knowledge in the face of new technology, the exact application of new knowledge is usually left to the individual. For example, a seminar may introduce a new synthetic material and explain its development, properties, and uses. The design engineer who will use the material to create a new product uses the information much differently than the engineer who will test the product once it is developed.

Employer selection of training providers for technical professionals varies depending on whether the information is proprietary, such as a new technology developed through in-house research and development; whether the expertise to deliver the training is available in-house; and whether the expertise is readily available and more cost-effective from outside sources.

When the training is proprietary or when it is more cost-effective, it is developed and delivered in-house. When an organization determines that it is more cost-effective to rely on outside sources to train its technical professionals, it is likely to turn to colleges and universities, professional associations, or original equipment manufacturers (OEMs) and other vendors.

The technical professional's ability to glean diverse applications from generic material makes course work, seminars, and symposia, such as those offered by colleges and universities, professional associations, and other public providers, a good alternative to in-house training. Aside from their course offerings, colleges and universities are the most frequent source of outside seminars, drawing about $41 million, or 35 percent of the $117 million spent annually by employers to provide seminars to their technical professionals.

OEMs and other vendors are another major source of training for technical professionals. They supplied approximately $175 million worth of off-the-shelf training materials, custom materials, and other training support services to technical professionals in 1987. Other sources of training (both in-house and outside) for technical professionals account for an additional $1.4 billion per year.

While specific curricula for technical professionals vary widely according to professional discipline and specific application, employer-provided training falls generally into three broad categories: (1) new technologies and processes within the specific field of study, (2) new applications of existing technologies, and (3) new product demonstrations.

Technical professionals are also likely to take safety training and hazard communication. Safety training includes the proper use of equipment; personal safety when using equipment; storage, handling, and disposal of hazardous materials; first aid; and even safety in the home. Hazard communication includes information on the harmful effects of hazardous materials found in the workplace; proper storage, handling, disposal, and clean-up of hazardous materials; the employer's responsibility for communicating with its employees about workplace hazards; how to recognize contamination, both in the workplace and on one's person; protective measures to take against occupational illnesses; and procedures to follow when inflicted with an illness or injury caused by hazardous materials.

Service-oriented curricula are more dependent on the particular industry than are curricula for manufacturing and include an in-depth study of the technical aspects of the service as it relates to sales, marketing, and potential new related services.

A growing number of manufacturing companies are presenting training in *integrated manufacturing* to their technical professionals. Integrated manufacturing covers all phases of manufacturing, including concept development, product design and development, production, distribution, and marketing. The principle of integrated manufacturing is to bring technical professionals together with production workers, sales and marketing personnel, and other members of the product team. The purpose is to reduce the time required to introduce new technologies and market new products, to improve efficiency and quality, and to encourage new innovations. Through training in integrated manufacturing technology, technical professionals can be responsible for more than one job or process rather than a single function or process, as was previously the case. This parallels cross-training and the trend toward work teams, which is becoming increasingly common among technicians and craft workers. It results in a more knowledgeable and versatile work force that is more responsive to organizational, technological, or industrial shifts.

Whether from manufacturing or service, technical professionals in supervisory positions also receive training in nontechnical areas, including labor relations, planning, delegating, problem solving, time management, interpersonal skills, materials management, team building, and leadership.

The average amount of time spent training technical professionals each year is difficult to determine for two reasons. First, much of the training for this group occurs away from the workplace. Second, training data are not readily available in organizations lacking direct management support.

The training managers interviewed for this book indicated a wide range in the amount of training provided to technical professionals. Those in industries with very rapidly changing technologies reported that their technical professionals spend at least ten days each year updating their skills. (The highest average was twenty-six days at a leading manufacturer of semiconductors and microprocessors.) Training managers in industries utilizing more stable technologies indicated a range from no professional development (an oil company) to five days of development per year (a metals manufacturer).

Technicians. Technicians include employees whose primary expertise lies in a particular technical specialty area. While technicians have a considerable depth of knowledge and highly developed skills in their areas of expertise, they generally lack the breadth of knowledge in the theoretical aspects of their specialties that is required of technical professionals. Although many technicians and technologists are graduates of four-year colleges, many have developed their skills and knowledge through technical or vocational schools, community colleges, or on-the-job training. After technical and nontechnical professionals, technicians are the most highly educated and well-trained employees in the American work force (see Table 1).

Technicians usually receive training that applies directly to their jobs. This training has its basis in theory but is focused more directly on the application of theory to the job than is training for technical professionals.

Employer selection of training providers for technicians follows the same pattern as for technical professionals. When

training is proprietary or when it is cost-effective, it is designed
and developed in-house. When it is more cost-effective to rely
on outside sources to train technicians, employers turn mainly
to colleges, universities, and professional associations.

Because of the nature of technician training, programs
sponsored by colleges (including two-year colleges), universities,
vocational schools, and professional associations are the most
frequent (but not the largest) source of training outside the companies themselves. Aside from course offerings, colleges and
universities draw 35 percent or about $24 million of the $68.9
million spent annually by employers to send their technicians
to seminars. In addition, vendors, especially OEMs, supply a
considerable amount of technician training and related support
materials. Of the more than $3.28 billion spent by employer
organizations each year for outside training and training support services, approximately $103.2 million goes for technician
training.

Training curricula for technicians are more job-specific
than curricula for technical professionals. However, most technician training is sequential and can be divided into three categories: (1) principles of new technologies (primarily equipment
and processing techniques), (2) new applications for existing
technologies, and (3) special courses required for licensing or
certification or refresher courses required for license renewal or
recertification.

Hull (1986) has proposed a detailed curriculum for what
he terms *Supertechs*. The curriculum is composed of three phases
of instruction, grouped functionally as basic core subjects, technical core subjects, and high-tech core subjects.

Hull's basic core includes subjects and courses designed
to provide a basis on which the remainder of the curriculum
can build. The technical core expands on the basic core, and
the high-tech core narrows courses to specific areas of advanced
study in the core area. New courses are added to the high-tech
core as new theories result in emerging technologies.

The goal of Hull's curriculum is to ensure that the technical worker has the knowledge and flexibility to work efficiently in
today's changing technological work force. Hull's model is valuable as an example of how a tiered curriculum can be developed.

Using the definitions of technical training and the target groups selected for this book suggests that training curricula for technicians vary widely and significantly, even at the basic level. Specifically, the curricula are industry-specific, assume high entry-level skills, and involve a strict level of supervision, especially at the second and third tiers. An example of the specific nature of the courses and of the higher entry skill and knowledge levels can be easily demonstrated by comparing sample courses for computer technicians and nursing candidates. Such a comparison is shown in Table 5.

**Table 5. Comparison of Basic Courses
for Computer Technicians and Nursing Students.**

| | Courses[a] | |
Generic Area	Computer Technician	Nursing Student
Mathematics	Metric conversion Algebra	Metric conversion Algebra
Science	Electricity Computer science	Chemistry Anatomy
Communication	Interpersonal skills	Interpersonal skills Psychology

[a]Not intended to be a complete basic-level curriculum.

While all courses can be factored into Hull's generic areas, the specific courses in the basic core imply high entry skill and knowledge requirements for the career fields noted and, quite probably, for most technician job categories. Second- and third-tier courses for technicians expand on the basic skills to include training in specific systems and/or equipment that will be used on the job. This factor further supports the more narrow, industry-focused approach to generic curricula for technicians.

Technicians also receive specific training in procedures required for successful job operation, especially if the procedures are regulated by a government agency. For example, a technician in a drug company receives training in operating and maintaining a clean room, laboratory technicians in hospitals receive training in maintaining sterile equipment or properly recording patient test results, and technicians in a nuclear power facility receive training in emergency shutdown and evacuation procedures.

Like technical professionals, technicians are generally required to take additional courses in safety hazard communication. Safety training includes proper use, maintenance, and/or repair of equipment; storage, handling, and disposal of hazardous materials; emergency procedures appropriate to the job (ranging from fire fighting to decontamination, first aid, and emergency evacuation procedures); personal safety (including maintaining a clean work area, using protective gear, and proper lifting to avoid back injuries, if appropriate); and safety in the home and on trips.

Hazard communication includes the proper labeling, storage, handling, and disposal of hazardous or potentially hazardous materials found in the workplace; employer responsibilities for hazard communication; posting of warning signs; identification of restricted areas; recognition of harmful effects of hazardous materials and symptoms exhibited by someone who encounters workplace contamination; procedures for avoiding occupational illnesses; and procedures to follow (and workers' rights) if an occupational illness is contracted from hazardous materials.

Technicians holding supervisory positions also receive nontechnical supervisory training that is similar to that offered to technical professionals.

The amount of time technicians spend in training varies widely, according to the job held, the value that the company places on training, and state and local certification (or licensing) requirements. Few statistics are available concerning the length of training specifically for technicians. However, one survey did examine the amount of training provided to first-line supervisors (including some technicians) in 125 manufacturing plants of varying sizes. The study showed courses ranging in length from 6 to 2,160 hours, with a median course length of 40 hours every six months (Harwood, 1978).

Data-Processing Technical Personnel. There are more than 1.5 million data-processing workers in the United States—more than 300,000 computer systems analysts, almost 500,000 computer programmers, more than 300,000 operators, and roughly 400,000 data-entry clerks. Of these, systems analysts are classified as technical professionals, while programmers fall into a hazy category somewhere between professionals and technicians, depending on their responsibilities. Operators and data-entry clerks are not technical workers according to our definition because they do not use theory in their work. They neither create nor manipulate the technology they use in their jobs. The computer is simply a job aide for them.

Data-processing personnel are a product of the information age. They build information systems and programs. They operate computers, compile and structure data, and input data into computers. Their primary product — information — may be sold to external sources or used internally as the raw material for institutional efficiency. Data-processing technical workers, such as systems analysts and computer scientists, perform research, development, and design functions outside the line structure of the institution. They are among the most highly educated and trained occupational groups in the American work force (see Table 6). Both systems analysts and programmers get at least as much education and training to qualify for their jobs as any of the major occupational categories shown in Table 1. Moreover, the proportion of systems analysts and programmers who are upgraded compares with professionals in the most intensively upgraded occupations.

Systems analysts get substantial preemployment education, usually in colleges or universities, to prepare for their jobs. Yet they rely on their employers to provide formal and informal training for upgrading their skills. Programmers use a balanced mix of schooling and employer-provided formal training and informal on-the-job training to qualify for their jobs and to upgrade their skills on the job.

With the miniaturization of computer capabilities and the spread of user-friendly technology, data-processing operations have become more dispersed. Data-processing operations are serving multiple roles as research and development centers, line departments, and service and training providers for the rest of the institution. In order to cope with dispersion, some employers

Table 6. Sources of Qualifying and Upgrading Training: Data-Processing Technical Personnel.

| | Percentage with Qualifying Training | | | | | Percentage with Upgrading | | | | |
| | | From | Employer-Based | | | | From | Employer-Based | | |
Occupational Group	Total	School	Formal	Informal		Total	School	Formal	Informal
Computer system analysts	94	70	27	45		64	16	37	25
Computer programmers	91	64	19	41		61	25	27	24

Source: Carey, 1985.

Note: Individual percentages can add up to more than the totals because some employees received training from more than one kind of source.

have established a new staff department, the information center, which serves as an intermediary between data-base managers and end users. The center provides "training, applications, and support to the computerized departments throughout a given company" (Kimmerling, 1986, p. 22). Even with user-friendly programs, communicating with the computer means learning a foreign language. Information centers perform a coordination and training function, helping end users produce spreadsheets and graphs as well as integrating hardware and applications between departments.

While advances in information-based technology have been the major source of changing skill requirements in many American jobs, data-processing occupations continue to be hardest hit by the whirlwind of changing skill requirements. The fact that data-processing employees are hit first and hardest by changes in information technologies accounts for the high degree of qualifying training and upgrading they receive, especially through employer-provided training programs. Technology simply moves too fast to wait for the schools to catch up.

Ironically, computer programs sometimes replace their creators. Jobs that originate with new technology are eventually simplified. For example, general-solution business applications such as VISICALC and LOTUS 1-2-3 are reducing the demand for computer programmers. It is no longer necessary for programmers to understand hardware architecture or design separate data structures for each application.

Interviews with a cross section of data-processing employees indicate that data-processing technical personnel generally have college degrees or have attended structured programs at technical schools to receive certification. Courses include managing information systems, computer design and analysis, auditing (of both systems and procedures, including security measures), and programming in specific computer languages, such as BASIC, FORTRAN, and COBOL.

Armed with basic education or certification, the aspiring data-processing worker usually enters the work force as a development specialist or a beginning programmer. Information managers who manage other computer professionals, as well as computer systems, report that although a college degree may be essential for movement into management in this field, support and mentoring from supervisors is often the most important ingredient for success on the job. This accounts for the relatively high level of informal on-the-job training among data-processing personnel shown in Table 6.

Skilled Trade (Blue-Collar) Technical Employees. The nation's blue-collar workers number almost 30 million and include craft workers and operations personnel, construction workers, repair workers, precision production workers, extractive workers (those in the mining industry), machine operators, assembly workers, transportation workers, and laborers. According to the definition used here, only the 11.8 million precision production, craft, and extractive workers, mechanics and repairers, and some machine operators and assembly workers qualify as technical workers. The remainder of the blue-collar work force is the labor pool from which new technical workers evolve.

With the exception of extractive workers and machine operators, roughly two-thirds of blue-collar technical workers get some kind of formal or informal preparation for their jobs, substantially less than the proportion of workers who get qualifying training in technician and technical professional careers. Skilled trade workers tend to rely on informal training on the job more than other occupations do for the qualifying training and upgrading they receive.

The purposes for training blue-collar technical workers vary considerably from those for training technical professionals and technicians. Depending on the course and the individual, skilled trade training may be provided for any of the following reasons: skill acquisition or update, certification or recertification, cross-training, or remediation of basic skills.

Skill acquisition training has traditionally been approached in two ways:

1. Through apprenticeship programs that combine classroom instruction with formal, supervised on-the-job training for a specific period of time (some programs last three years

or more) before the apprentice is granted journeyman status and permitted to work independently
2. Through coaching and other informal on-the-job programs in which a new employee learns a job by watching an expe-- rienced employee perform a task, then practicing it until he or she can perform in the job without supervision

Many companies, especially those in high-tech industries, are beginning to formalize skill acquisition and update training for skilled trade workers by using simulators and other advanced learning technologies in an effort to increase control and uni- formity of training while reducing time lost from the job. This trend is developing as a result of inconsistent training received through informal on-the-job training programs and increased pressure on training and line personnel to increase quality and productivity through better use of human resources.

When certification or licensing (or recertification or re- licensing) is the training goal, corporate training strategy often includes a two-track (high-tech, low-tech) course. Workers in high-tech jobs are more likely to receive training from outside sources. This is especially true for jobs requiring a specific num- ber of hours or continuing education units (CEUs) for recerti- fication or certification at a higher level of proficiency. Employees in low-tech jobs are more likely to receive their recertification training through in-house programs.

Cross-training is often provided on-site as a means of ex- panding the range of skills and knowledge within a work area. It is becoming more prevalent in companies requiring a versa- tile work force that is more responsive to changes in the work- place or industry.

Remediation is becoming a greater issue for employers for the following reasons:

•   Labor shortages caused by the aging U.S. work force re- quire employers to hire individuals that formerly would have been considered unqualified.
•   Advancing technologies now require higher levels of basic skills than were required for older, less complex technologies.

- The United States is now operating in a global economy
  that is more competitive and shifting more rapidly than
  ever before.

As more companies respond to the need for remediation, many
are finding that their needs are best met by outside contracting
to public and private sources.

    Sources of training for blue-collar technical workers are
more diverse but better balanced than those for either technical
professionals or technicians. OEM training is a vital source when
the training goal is skill acquisition or update on new processes
or equipment. The rationale behind OEM training is that the
manufacturer has a better understanding of equipment, processes, and procedures than any other source and is therefore
more qualified to conduct the training. Many companies purchase OEM training as a part of the acquisition cost of new
equipment.

    Local colleges, vocational schools, and trade associations
are major sources for certification and licensing training. Local
colleges, local school districts, and public sources, such as those
resulting from the Job Training Partnership Act, are key providers for remediation and skill acquisition.

    Skilled trade workers pursue a tiered course of study that
is similar in structure to that proposed for technicians. The three
tiers of their training include (1) a basic skills core, (2) a technical
core, and (3) an applied technical core.

    The basic skills core provides workers with an understand-
ing of and an aptitude for mathematics, science, and communication. The technical core provides an introduction to the
principles involved in areas such as electricity, mechanics, computers, gauging and measurement, thermal systems, machining,
and engines and power systems. With the exception of apprenticeship programs, much of the training in the first two tiers
takes place away from the job site, on the individual's time, and
at the individual's expense. Many employers require their employees to have completed courses through at least the second
tier prior to employment.

    The applied technical core provides workers with an un-
derstanding of how to apply the principles learned in the second

tier to a specific job. Courses in this tier place heavy emphasis on developing and refining the skills required on the job. The majority of instruction in this tier is devoted to demonstration, coaching, and practice.

As workers progress in skill level and experience, they can take additional courses intended to upgrade skills for new or advancing technologies. These courses can also be factored into a tiered structure but begin on a higher level. The emphasis throughout the advanced-level courses is on skill enhancement rather than skill development.

Courses in all areas can deal with specific equipment or with systems, depending on the nature of the job and the employer's needs. (Cross-training and pay-for-knowledge programs, for example, are oriented more toward systems than specific equipment.)

In addition to job-specific training, skilled trade workers receive the same courses in safety and hazard communication that are provided to technicians. The key difference, if any, is that safety programs may be tailored to emphasize those safety aspects and procedures that are most important to specific jobs.

Foremen, lead workers, and other first-line supervisors also receive a core of nontechnical courses in supervisory skills.

As with technician training, the amount of time spent in training blue-collar technical workers varies widely. For example, one hazard communication program reportedly takes as little as three hours to complete, whereas the Aluminum Company of America's apprenticeship program is 6,000 hours with an approximate one-third/two-thirds split between classroom training and on-the-job training. Overall, data remain sketchy for craft personnel because despite the movement to formalize training for this group, much training remains informal and is therefore not reported as a training occurrence.

Evolution of the Technical Work Force

The future of technical jobs is closely linked to the process of technological change itself. Technical skill requirements are continuously being driven upward by new technology, and the growth in technical jobs follows a similar pattern. As new technology becomes a substitute for human labor, eliminating tasks or reconfiguring them into fewer jobs that combine more highly skilled labor with more machine capital, the evolution of technical work assumes the form of a pyramid. Many labor-intensive and less productive jobs are restructured into a few capital- and knowledge-intensive jobs that are more productive.

Projections of occupational growth to the year 2000 from the Bureau of Labor Statistics (see Table 7) reflect that pyramid pattern by demonstrating the occupations in the economy that will undergo significant growth or decline. Depending on the economic scenario, the number of technical jobs is projected to increase from 21 to 32 percent in the next twelve years. The same projections for jobs in the economy as a whole are considerably lower, ranging from 13 to 23 percent. Projected job growth is especially notable among technical professionals, and as is true among all workers, education and training and development are the keys to securing these jobs. Even a casual review of the projections by the Bureau of Labor Statistics shown in Table 7 reveals the necessary escalation of skill and productivity as jobs evolve upward in the technical hierarchy.

Table 7. Employment Growth, 1986–2000.

Occupation	Low Growth Path (Percentage)	High Growth Path (Percentage)
Scientists	+ 37	+ 52
Engineers	+ 23	+ 37
Technicians	+ 31	+ 43
Craft	+ 12	+ 23
Mechanics and repairers	+ 8	+ 19
Precision manufacturing workers	− 2	+ 9
Machine operators	− 10	+ 1
Assemblers	− 12	0

Source: Carey, 1985.

Conclusion

In industries that require technical workers, there is a large and growing investment in the continuous updating and upgrading of technical skills. This investment is driven by necessity.

Technical workers have unique training needs that are defined by technical specialty, the emergence of new technology, and safety or regulatory requirements.

Currently, technical workers receive the lion's share of the corporate training dollar. With rapidly changing technology and competitive pressures to reduce cycle time, that investment will only grow.

CHAPTER 2

How Technical Training
Systems Work

There is growing consensus among employer organizations that technical training is absolutely critical for successful operation within an economic environment characterized by rapidly advancing technology and complexity. However, although technical training is generally considered to be most effective when it is closely aligned with organizational operations and when it is an integrated part of the corporate strategic planning process, there is no consensus among employers as to the optimal structure and organization for technical training. Disagreements revolve around how the technical training function should be structured, under which corporate function or discipline it should be organized, what degree of participation it should have in overall corporate planning, and what relationship it should have with line operations.

How an employer's technical training system is structured and organized determines how well such training supports the organization's mission and objectives. Structure and organization determine the degree of interaction among technical training, line operations, and human resource activities. They dictate whether technical training will be a primary consideration as senior-level management formulates corporate strategies or whether it will be relegated to the organizational fringes, with no real impact on strategic planning and decision making. Depending upon how technical training is structured and organized, it can assist in improving specific operational areas that have a direct impact on the entire organization, including production or manufacturing. The right structure and organization can also enable technical training personnel to focus their resources on specific activities that are key to an organization's success.

Careful attention to the technical training system and its structure and organization is paramount if it is to become a successful conduit for the skills and knowledge necessary for the technical work force to accomplish its mission and objectives. Ultimately, with the right structure and organization, technical training can play a dominant role in reducing a company's operating costs, increasing productivity, reducing scrap and waste, decreasing equipment downtime, decreasing employee turnover, and reducing work-related accidents.

This chapter discusses technical training systems as they have developed and are in use today within employer organizations in the United States. It also examines the factors that have contributed to employers' decisions concerning what type of technical training system and structure is most appropriate for their organizations. Those factors include the nature of the product and industry, corporate culture, strategic goals, technical target groups, and whether the company is a division or subsidiary of a larger organization (in which case, the type of technical training system may be specified by the parent organization).

Technical Training Structure

Technical training structure — how the technical training is controlled — and organization — where it is located — have a great deal to do with how and how well the function operates. No single technical training system is appropriate for all organizations. Rather, technical training structure and organization usually depend upon the characteristics of the employees to be trained, the nature of the industry and product or service, the state of technology in the workplace, and the unique needs imposed by specialized plant operations within the organization. Generally, there are three ways in which employers can structure their technical training functions: (1) centrally, (2) decentrally, or (3) a combination of the two.

Technical Training Structure: Centralized. Technical training is considered centralized when the function is controlled and/ or coordinated from a single location within the organization. When technical training is completely centralized, the company headquarters controls or coordinates the needs analysis, design, development, delivery, and evaluation of technical training for all employees throughout the organization. That is not to say, however, that control of technical training must be at the highest organizational level to be considered centralized. For example, diverse subsidiaries of a holding company generally have separate headquarters that oversee their respective operations with a great deal of autonomy. Usually each subsidiary's headquarters also exercises control over its own technical training function; such a structure constitutes centralized training.

There are several advantages to having centralized control of technical training, especially in organizations with similar operations among various divisions and plants. In such cases, a centralized training structure avoids a duplication of effort among similar facilities and reduces overall training costs through the consolidation of training resources such as staff, facilities, equipment, and materials. This is especially critical in certain high-technology organizations in which complex and expensive simulators or computer-based systems are necessary for training. Training efforts within the organization's various operations can be coordinated to optimize training resource usage and to enlarge the experience base from which training can be drawn. A centralized training function also serves as a cross-pollination mechanism through which employees from each facility learn from the experiences of others.

Centralization ensures that training throughout the organization is uniform and that it supports corporate strategic goals and special top-level priorities such as safety, quality, or employee work teams. It also facilitates the introduction of new product or processing technologies that will have an impact on the entire organization. Centralized control of technical training appears to be particularly beneficial in organizations that are highly regulated, where a product must be produced to exacting standards, or where safety is a critical factor of production.

Niagara Mohawk is an energy company with diversified interests and resources in coal, nuclear energy, and natural gas. It is the chief supplier of electricity to 1.5 million customers from Lake Erie to New England. It also provides natural gas to 450,000 customers in central, eastern, and northern New York State and provides electricity and gas transmission services to other utilities.

Since Niagara Mohawk is a utility company involving a potentially dangerous work environment that includes nuclear- and fossil-fuel-generated power and natural gas transmission, it is under very strict regulation from the New York Public Utilities Commission as well as the federal Nuclear Regulatory Commission, the Occupational Safety and Health Administration, and the Environmental Protection Agency. When Niagara Mohawk's management conducts its strategic planning and identifies strategic goals, it considers its regulatory requirements along with other key issues, including providing quality and reliable service. To best achieve its corporate strategies, the company has made technical training a priority and has established it as a centrally controlled operation. Niagara Mohawk's corporate training staff provides training at both headquarters and on-site facilities throughout the service territory. With centralized control, the company ensures that technical training is uniform in focus and quality, that it meets all regulatory requirements, and that it provides the skills necessary for employees to provide safe, high-quality, reliable power and natural gas service.

As in the Niagara Mohawk example, a centrally controlled technical training function may have decentralized training delivery. Under a pure central structure, corporate training programs are designed at a central location. An organization may determine, however, that training can be accomplished more effectively if delivered by the central staff *decentrally* at the individual plants. Nevertheless, organizations still view this as centralized training because it is controlled and coordinated centrally and delivered by the central training staff.

Technical Training Structure: Decentralized. Centralized control over technical training is not well suited to all organizations. Some companies have found a centralized structure to

be inefficient and cumbersome when unique products or processes create specialized missions among their facilities or operating units. In such cases, a centralized structure is too far removed
from line operations to be effective, and a decentralized structure
may be preferable.

Technical training systems are considered decentralized
when control over training functions is delegated to a lower
organizational level and there is no common point of coordination among separate facilities or training entities. A decentralized structure works well in organizations producing a diverse
array of products or using several different processing methods
or levels of technology. It is prevalent in organizations that
have divisions that manufacture products for entirely different
industries. In such cases, each division is provided a great deal
of autonomy over production and technical training. A decentralized structure places technical training closer to line operations and allows it to develop closer relationships with the
operations personnel from whom technical workers must draw
their expertise.

Federal Express, one of the largest transporters of overnight packages, exemplifies a decentralized technical training
structure within an organization having one product but involving several unique processes. Essentially, the organization's work
force is involved in three distinctly different operations: flight
operations, which encompasses the operation of the company's
air fleet; ground operations, which involves the maintenance
of aircraft, select facilities, and package-handling equipment and
aircraft interface (fueling, towing, deicing); and customer support, which includes package handling, courier delivery, and
customer service. Since each operation requires a different skill
and knowledge base, Federal Express has decentralized its technical training into three main functions corresponding to the
three types of operations: flight operations training, maintenance
and engineering training, and domestic ground operations training. Decentralization allows each technical training function to
establish a training staff that designs, develops, and delivers
training programs that are tailored to meet the specific needs
of its operational area.

Siemens USA, a producer and marketer of electronics and electrical equipment, offers an example of a decentralized technical training structure within an organization with completely autonomous divisions. The company's organization, which parallels that of its parent, Siemens AG of Germany, consists of the following divisions: Siemens Communications Systems, a provider of networking, switching, and transmission equipment; Siemens Medical Systems, a provider of medical electronic diagnostic and therapeutic equipment and systems; Siemens Energy and Automation Systems, a provider of electrical and electronic equipment for the construction, industrial, and utility markets; Siemens Components, a producer of high-quality integrated circuits; Siemens KWU, a producer of power generation equipment and nuclear fuels; and Siemens Information Systems, a provider of advanced information products and systems and private communication systems.

Siemens USA has completely decentralized its operations, believing that each division is the most knowledgeable and best equipped to make production and marketing decisions concerning its products. For the same reason, each division is responsible for its own technical training function. Within each division, the technical training structure ranges from centralized control and coordination, such as at Siemens Medical Systems (because of its highly complex and state-of-the-art medical equipment) to completely decentralized control, such as at Siemens Energy and Automation Systems (because of the unique products and processes of its operating departments). In fact, in the latter case, each *department* has complete responsibility for its own technical training. Within Siemens USA, there is no coordination of either operational or technical training activities among the divisions.

A decentralized structure is inefficient in organizations where some products or processes are similar within a division or department or among several facilities. It is also more difficult to link technical training to the mission and strategies of the high-level organization and for corporate management to provide coordination. Decentralized structure is therefore more susceptible to the influence of local management and more difficult to control and monitor in terms of supporting the company's overall strategies and other top-level priorities.

Technical Training Structure: Combination of Centralized and Decentralized. Some companies have chosen to combine parts of both centralized and decentralized training structures. Training is controlled or coordinated from a single point for specific subject matter, phases of training, and/or target groups. All other technical training operations are decentralized to lower-level organizational entities to better address the company's products, processes, or procedures. This structure provides advantages in that common courses or training for specific groups can be controlled centrally while allowing local facilities the latitude they require to meet the needs of unique processes, procedures, or equipment.

Many companies, for example, have chosen to centralize control over design and development of safety and hazard communication courses, while allowing local plants to tailor the courses and deliver them to meet their local needs. Others have centralized all training for technical professionals in the belief that much of this training involves common, theoretical content that can then be tailored to individual applications on the job; yet the same companies have decentralized training for craft workers so that plants can train those workers in the vagaries of local equipment.

Frito-Lay, Inc., a large producer of snack foods, is one example of an organization with a combination of centralized and decentralized technical training within the five phases of training. All technical training is designed, developed, and administered centrally by a training staff located at the company's headquarters. Frito-Lay's forty individual plants have on-site training staffs that deliver the training that is designed and delivered by members of the central staff. Although the central and plant training staffs work together, there is no direct organizational link between the two. By combining elements of both the centralized and decentralized training structures, Frito-Lay achieves the benefits of both systems. Central design and development ensures that all corporate goals and special programs are adequately supported in the training. It increases efficiency through the consolidation of all design and development activities within a single training staff. Decentralized delivery allows individual plants to customize courses in response to specific requirements and is consistent with Frito-Lay's Self-Reliance Program, which promotes increased autonomy at the plants. Decentralized training delivery also increases the amount of hands-on training, while at the same time reducing the amount of time required away from the job for training.

Polaroid, a designer, manufacturer, and marketer of instant-image products, exemplifies an organization with a combination of centralized and decentralized technical training among its target groups. Technical training for technical professionals and technicians is designed, developed, and delivered centrally at the company's headquarters facility. Centralized training is considered best for these target groups because (1) the subject matter involves the latest product and process technologies, which require rapid dissemination throughout the organization, and (2) the subject matter is often not specific to any one plant or process. Polaroid's training for skilled trade workers is mostly decentralized, however, because their training is primarily plant-specific. Although these target groups are trained under different structures, training for each group is considered equally important and receives equal management support and funding.

Despite the apparent advantages of a combined structure, a major disadvantage is the difficulty of coordination between headquarters and local plants. Of the training managers interviewed, several indicated that it was difficult to determine the dividing line between centralized and decentralized training. In such cases, the managers stated that there was a tendency for local facilities to act independently and not take advantage of course offerings and expertise available through the central training staff. Most managers stressed the need for some degree of coordination between central training operations and individual training units at local sites.

Trends in Training Structure. Despite a large degree of decentralization still found in technical training, there appears to be a clear trend toward centralizing control over the design and development of technical courses. Only delivery appears to be remaining truly decentralized, and this occurs primarily with technicians and craft workers. Of the thirty-three training managers interviewed for our study, eighteen indicated either that the technical training function is now centrally controlled and/or coordinated or that it is in the process of being repositioned to centralize control or coordination for at least a portion of technical training. This appears to be the case regardless of economic sector (see Table 8). Moreover, in a 1987 survey of companies, the Work in America Institute found that there is a trend toward centralizing control over the training function generally as a means of providing, brokering, and/or maintaining quality control over training programs.

Table 8. Breakdown of Study Participants by Structure.

	Sector		
Structure	Manufacturing	Service	Total[b]
Centralized[a]	12	8	20
Decentralized	12	4	16

[a]Or repositioning for centralized control and/or coordination.
[b]Some companies are counted twice because they engage in both manufacturing and service.

Organization of Technical Training

A review of corporate organizational charts reveals that there are several ways to position technical training within an organization. The most prevalent methods are to position it under human resources or personnel or to integrate it within line operations, such as manufacturing or production. A few companies, primarily those using a combination of centralized and decentralized technical training, have positioned the centralized portion beneath human resources and the decentralized portion within plant line operations. In rare situations, technical training is positioned as an autonomous function, not directly linked to other corporate functions. In any case, the exact position of technical training within the organization depends on the corporate mission and the perceived role of training in that mission.

One of the most common locations of technical training in corporate hierarchies is within the personnel or human resource function. Companies with this type of organization believe that it facilitates the coordination of technical training with other types of training and human resource functions. This is especially important in companies that use technical training as a basis for promotion or compensation. Also, since many personnel and human resource functions are already linked to operational strategies, placing technical training under those functions links it more closely to the strategies. This enhances training's ability to manage and monitor outcomes in terms of their relationship to the corporate mission and strategies.

Despite these advantages, however, some companies believe that placing technical training in personnel or human reources leaves it too far from line operations and hampers its ability to meet the company's operational needs. They also assert that placement in personnel or human resources allows technical training to be easily influenced or controlled by people with little or no understanding of it. Companies desiring a closer link to the line and/or desiring control by experienced line personnel frequently choose to place technical training within operations. These companies find it easier to evaluate outcomes in terms of specific target groups.

Carrier Corporation is the world's leading manufacturer of heating, ventilation, and air-conditioning equipment. Centralized for the analysis, design, development, and delivery of technical training, Carrier's technical training function is located within "industrial relations" under "manufacturing." This organization provides the advantage of working closely with line personnel to design, develop, and deliver training that meets the needs of its apprentice and technical supervisory programs as well as its cross-training, retraining, and new technology training and remediation programs.

But organizing technical training under line operations can lead to difficulties in linking training to a company's operating strategies and to the tendency for training to be overshadowed by pressing production needs. Carrier has tackled the problem by including the training manager on the corporate planning council. The training manager is therefore aware of all plans for expansion, reduction, or other operational changes well in advance of their initiation. Thus the manager has adequate time to develop training plans and courses that directly support operational goals. Carrier uses one-year and five-year plans that include new equipment, personnel, and marketing planning strategies. Suggestions made by the training department can also be incorporated in the planning process and implemented during execution of the plans. As a result, all training conducted at Carrier directly supports the company's strategic goals.

Staffing Technical Training

Internal Staffing. Of equal importance to structure and organization are issues surrounding the staffing of the technical training function. All organizations surveyed for this book met their staffing needs by hiring and using one or a combination of the following:

- Individuals with adult learning backgrounds
- Individuals with technical backgrounds
- Individuals with technical *and* adult learning backgrounds
- Teams comprised of one individual with a technical background and one with an adult learning background

Companies that hire *individuals with adult learning backgrounds* are seeking the expertise these people bring in terms of training context. Their ability to design programs for learning transfer makes adult learning experts valuable to many organizations. One drawback to using adult learning experts, however, is that most do not have a thorough understanding of technical processes and procedures for which they must design training. Their lack of expertise makes them less able to design courses with highly technical content and less credible when presenting training to participants who are more knowledgeable than they in the subject area. Also, in companies in which training is a rotational duty rather than a career track, dedicated trainers are less flexible and therefore less desirable than technical personnel because they cannot rotate into line positions.

A more common approach to staffing is to use people who are experienced in operations, that is, *individuals with technical backgrounds.* Companies using this approach believe that staffing technical training with experienced technical personnel is preferable for two reasons. First, technical personnel have a thorough understanding of the subject matter and can reduce the amount of time required for design and development. Second, their experience enables them to relate better to the needs of the participants during delivery. However, subject matter experts require training in adult learning theory and stand-up training techniques as a minimum before they can adequately present training. If they are to design training as well, they require considerably more background in adult learning and design techniques. Another drawback to developing line personnel as trainers is that it can take well over a year to teach them to develop and conduct training, and experienced line personnel often do not want to make that type of commitment.

Because of the extensive investment involved in training operations personnel to staff the technical training function, selection procedures are critical for Niagara Mohawk. The company has addressed these issues by using a combination of the roles and competencies described in ASTD's *Models for Excellence* (1983) and the well-known Kepner Trego selection package as a basis for determining job descriptions for selection. After posting a vacancy, the training director screens applications to review the applicants' experience levels in the desired content area, then reviews them again to narrow the number of candidates according to weighted criteria developed as part of the job description. Those identified as finalists present exercises in front of a jury of incumbents from the training staff. Final selection is based on the individual's technical expertise, communication skills, personality, and attitude.

After selection, the new instructor begins an intense train-the-trainer process that starts immediately after his or her selection and ends after one year of employment in training. This training process includes four steps: (1) a train-the-trainer session (which may be offered in-house or through Cornell University), (2) a teaming experience with an experienced training employee who coaches the new instructor through several training sessions, (3) an instructor improvement evaluation to identify major strengths and weaknesses, and (4) an annual performance evaluation that is given one year from the date the instructor began in the position (not from the date of hire). Only after one year as an instructor is the individual eligible for promotion, and only then can he or she begin to design or develop courses.

Most training managers interviewed for this book stated that their preference for a training staff member is an *individual with both a technical background and an adult learning background.* However, most managers also agreed that such a combination is difficult to find and equally difficult to retain.

An approach used by several companies is a *team approach* in which an individual with an adult learning background works with a subject matter expert (and sometimes a media or computer expert). Teaming permits both technical expertise and adult learning theory to be incorporated in the training. This system may be the most efficient and cost-effective approach to staffing because it permits part-time or rotating use of line personnel on an as-needed basis. It also allows adult learning specialists to provide an appropriate context for course content. With this approach, delivery is usually provided by line personnel.

Northern Telecom Inc. is a wholly owned U.S. subsidiary of Canadian-based Northern Telecom, Ltd., the world's largest supplier of information management systems. Technical courses provided by Northern Telecom's Integrated Network Systems Division, which produces telecommunications switching equipment, are developed by means of a three-person approach. A course "prime designate" is an individual with an operations background who is responsible for the overall course content. An individual with adult learning expertise is responsible for developing an appropriate context for the learning populations, and a media specialist develops all accompanying media. The training director at Northern Telecom believes that the team approach is the most efficient and cost-effective means of developing training that not only transfers to the job but keeps abreast of the rapidly changing technology required by the telecommunications industry.

External Training Providers. Regardless of staffing arrangements, most companies have indicated that at some point, they have relied on outside suppliers to meet their training needs. Though the supplier selected depends heavily on a company's staffing level, the type of program required, and the target group for which the training is intended, companies turn to three major sources of outside providers:

1. Colleges, universities, and professional associations
2. Original equipment manufacturers
3. Other vendors, including consultants and producers of commercially available training packages

Colleges, universities, and professional associations are a major source of outside training for technical professionals, especially scientists and engineers. Because most training for technical professionals is intended to update skills and knowledge about advancing or new technologies but leave the exact application of the technology to the individual on the job, programs offered by colleges, universities, and professional associations are good alternatives to developing in-house curricula in nonproprietary subjects for technical professionals.

Colleges and universities are also a frequent source of supplemental upgrading training for technicians, who require a mix of theory and application to upgrade their job skills.

Skilled trade workers are more likely to attend training sponsored by local colleges, vocational-technical schools, and professional groups. This is especially true for jobs requiring a specific number of hours or continuing education units for recertification or certification at a higher level of proficiency.

OEMs are another widely used outside training provider, especially when the training goal is skill acquisition on a new system, process, or procedure. Many companies purchase OEM training as part of the acquisition cost of new equipment. For example, Carrier Corporation absorbs OEM and other training costs for equipment operators and maintenance personnel as part of the cost of new equipment.

A third major outside source for employee training is vendors, including consultants and producers of commercially available training packages. Despite the existence of an in-house technical training staff, Ford Motor Company depends on outside suppliers for much of its training. Ford's internal training staff members act primarily as project managers for courses and programs that consultants and/or local colleges and universities have provided. The use of external providers will be explored more fully in Chapter Three.

Technical Training and Corporate Strategies

The current trend toward an increasingly close alliance between technical training and line operations has resulted from the active role of technical training in supporting corporations as they refocused their strategies and restructured in response to a changing U.S. economic environment. This active role has enhanced technical training's credibility and reputation as well as elevated its prominence among other corporate functions. Training has also undergone its own transformation, becoming more centralized in order to support corporate strategies and missions more effectively.

The dramatic transformation of the U.S. corporate operating environment has caused many of the changes in corporate organizations. Almost all industries and companies have been affected to some extent by rapidly changing technologies. Their products, services, and processes must be updated more frequently to keep abreast of proliferating technologies and innovations. In many cases, corporate structures and operations have become completely driven by technology. Organizations have also become subject to fierce competition as the U.S. economy has become increasingly global. U.S. companies have been forced to accelerate product development cycles and impose greater efficiencies to compete successfully against the lower-wage, high-growth, off-shore economies. At the same time, a growing consumer awareness has increased the demand for improved product quality, reliability, and styling. This issue has become an almost universal corporate priority. Escalating costs caused by greater operating complexities, product litigation, expanding safety and environmental regulations, and tremendous increases in employee benefit costs have generated additional obstacles for U.S. companies. Together, these factors have a synergistic relationship that has prompted most organizations to reexamine their operations, products, and missions.

During the process of adapting missions, operations, and products to changing economic conditions, companies have been developing new attitudes toward the work force. Increasingly, they view employees as a valuable and renewable resource that is critical to operations. Regardless of the degree of technology involved in their operations, most organizations are discovering that a skilled and motivated work force that is dedicated to excellence is essential to surmounting the obstacles in today's economy. They are also discovering that employees are most effective when given greater responsibility and increased authority over their work assignments.

Whether an organization responds to these environmental factors by streamlining or modifying its structure, modernizing or replacing its plant and equipment, or improving or expanding its product lines, technical training is playing an ever-increasing role in the execution of the changes. It has been flexible in adapting to the diversity of product and process technologies and to the needs of a heterogeneous technical work force with a variety of organizational structures, staff expertise, training methodologies, and subject matter.

In most organizations, technical training supports most or all corporate strategic goals. It supports new product or manufacturing technologies by providing workers with the requisite skills and knowledge levels. These same skills boost productivity and efficiency and improve product quality. A skilled work force also reduces operating costs by minimizing waste, operating deficiencies, manufacturing variances, and equipment downtime. In addition, technical training promotes safety when its curricula address hazardous materials and processes. Moreover, it supports, although less directly, strategic goals such as enhancing shareholder value by promoting increased productivity and greater efficiencies.

The visibility and contribution of technical training to corporate operations vary significantly, depending upon the specific organization and perceived value of the function. Some organizations, like Northern Telecom, believe that training is crucial enough to be integrated into line operations at one of its plants.

Northern Telecom's Rancho Bernardo plant, which produces application-specific integrated circuit components, had not been operating at an optimal level of productivity or product quality. Following an examination of plant operations, the plant managers decided to restructure the plant under the new strategic goal of becoming the premier producer of semiconductors. The managers opted for work teams, with each responsible for a specific workstation within a primary plant activity: fabrication, testing, or assembly. Each work team was given the authority to obtain all resources necessary to accomplish any task, goal, or objective. Work teams were also responsible for selecting new employees for the team and for providing a work team orientation program.

From the start, the plant managers recognized the absolute necessity for a technical training system that provided advanced skills and knowledge, as well as the equipment and procedure training required for each team member to operate, troubleshoot, and maintain each piece of equipment in the team's workstation. Additionally, each team member had to keep abreast of the latest product and manufacturing technologies affecting the workstation. To obtain the maximum flexibility and understanding of each work team's unique training requirements, technical training was included as one of the work team's functional responsibilities. Each team became responsible for identifying and analyzing its training needs, structuring a training program, selecting and developing a team trainer, and conducting the training.

At the Rancho Bernardo plant, technical training has been completely incorporated into the work team line operations. This is considered the most effective way of supporting plant operations by providing a highly skilled work force, which in turn supports the plant's main strategy of becoming the preeminent semiconductor producer. Such a structure enables training to pinpoint operational discrepancies accurately and to respond to those problems with remedial training almost immediately. The structure also ensures that new product and process technologies are disseminated more quickly and that related training support is established concurrently.

In some organizations, the technical training function is represented by someone who actively participates in the corporate-level strategic planning process. The extent of involvement depends on the individual company and ranges from acting as an observer of the strategic planning proceedings to being an active proponent who ensures that all strategic goals include a training perspective.

At Frito-Lay, Inc., technical training is directly involved in the corporate strategic planning process. The company's senior management periodically convenes planning and strategy sessions to establish strategic goals for the next three to five years. Generally, the goals encompass overall corporate direction and more specific manufacturing and production objectives. A representative from the company's central technical training function attends these sessions and provides input concerning the potential impact of the proposed goals and objectives on both training and the work force. Although not directly linked with individual plant trainers, the central training staff maintains a continual interface with site trainers to ensure that their feedback receives proper consideration in the strategy planning process. Once specific goals and objectives receive approval and are implemented, the central technical training function establishes training goals and objectives that correspond to the corporate strategic goals and serve as guidelines for future training efforts.

Some organizations, such as Motorola, have elected to establish a technical training operation that is completely linked to corporate strategies. The Motorola Training and Education Center is a centrally controlled employee training and education organization that is charged with improving individual and organizational performance and productivity throughout the organization. The center accomplishes its training at a central state-of-the-art facility, located near corporate headquarters and at five regional facilities, three of which are located in the United States and two overseas. As mandated by the center's mission statement, all training provided by the center supports or addresses current corporate strategic goals, such as product quality, inventory reduction, and customer service.

The job of identifying or updating corporate strategic goals and the associated training requirements is the responsibility of several senior-level committees. First, the Motorola Training and Education Center's advisory board, consisting of the company's senior executives, including its chairman, meets twice a year to update and chart the corporate strategic plan, determine a general training direction to support the plan, and develop a general budget for each of five broad functional areas. Next, the Motorola Training and Education Center's five functional advisory councils, representing engineering, manufacturing/materials, marketing, personnel, and sales, meet to translate the executive advisory board's training guidance into specific plans for each of their respective functional areas. Each functional advisory council meets quarterly to determine and prioritize specific training requirements for its area. Finally, the Motorola Training and Education Center designs and develops training programs and courses based on the specific guidelines and parameters provided by the five councils.

Organizations that involve technical training in the strategic planning process do so in the belief that the corporation is better served overall by the training function. In times of budgetary constraints and limited resources, it is also the most effective means for targeting training efforts toward specific operational problems or corporate opportunities. Finally, by involving technical training in the strategic planning process, training personnel become aware of operational problems or new equipment purchases sooner and are able to respond more quickly with the most appropriate training programs.

Conclusion

As workplace technologies change and U.S. businesses compete more and more in a global economy, corporate managers are becoming more aggressive in linking their technical training requirements to the corporate strategic goals. In this effort, they are carefully weighing the organization's needs so that technical training can be structured and organized to contribute more actively to meeting corporate strategies.

Technical training managers within organizations are also carefully identifying the specific needs of each target population within organizations to ensure that the training provided is appropriate, timely, and consistent with the companies' overall business goals.

CHAPTER 3

How Technical Training Is Provided

In today's world of work, the metalsmith is now a metallurgical technician; the engineer's aide is a technologist; and the lathe operator of old monitors and programs machining cells that contain an array of computer-controlled machine tools and robotic material-handling devices. Technological changes are driving the evolution of occupations, compelling employees to learn new skills in order to adapt to new roles and work in new ways. This means that entry-level workers must come to a prospective employer with an increasingly sophisticated repertoire of skills. And veteran employees must often scramble to upgrade their skills just to keep their jobs.

Technological changes are also shifting the employer perspective on technical training. While in the past most employers recognized the importance of technical training, they often had the luxury of providing or facilitating their workers' training over an extended time period. Now, however, today's innovation is tomorrow's outdated equipment. To stay competitive, employers are discovering that they must keep their technical work force up-to-date because there is much to win but still more to lose if their workers do not have the necessary technical skills. Productivity and a healthy bottom line are at risk if a technical work force cannot acquire the skills it needs in a timely manner.

The good news is that there are many who can assist in the design, development, and delivery of up-to-date skills. Often employers themselves have the in-house capability to provide training. Even when they do not, however, many other training providers are available to come to their aid.

Employer investment in overall training is large. About $210 billion is spent annually on formal and informal training. Research conducted for this book, as well as the work of others, including the Bureau of Labor Statistics, shows that about 30 percent of that $210 billion is spent on technical training.

Because employers cannot provide all the necessary training with an in-house staff, they have formed cooperative ventures with training providers. Such cooperation between employers and outside providers is critical for ensuring that the quality of technical training is high and that the delivery of technical training is available, efficient, and timely. By working together, employers and outside providers of training can provide a rapidly changing work force with the skills and knowledge required to keep America's competitive position strong. Cooperation does not always come easily, however, and employers and outside providers must work to forge meaningful partnerships that are flexible, efficient, and innovative.

To improve the quality and efficiency of technical training, employers are faced with several challenges:

- They must understand how and when technical workers get their training.
- They must know who the providers of technical training are.
- They must learn how to interact with those providers to improve the quality, efficiency, and delivery of training.

This chapter attempts to help employers meet those challenges.

Technical Training Patterns

There are discernible patterns in the technical training that each target group receives. The findings discussed in this chapter were calculated by using data from Bureau of Labor Statistics Bulletin #2226 by Max Carey (Carey, 1985) as a base. It is possible to trace the amount of training that technical professionals, technicians, and skilled trade workers receive and the institutions that most often provide the training. Moreover, each target group receives its qualifying training and upgrading training in distinctive patterns that result from differences in skill requirements, skills levels, and certification or licensing requirements.

Nevertheless, some generalities are evident. All workers tend to receive more training to qualify for their jobs than they do to upgrade their skills. For technical workers in particular, between 67 and 79 percent of technical professionals and technicians receive more qualifying training than upgrading training. Approximately 50 to 75 percent of technical professionals and technicians participate in upgrading training, but fewer than 50 percent of skilled trade workers participate in skill upgrading.

Rapid shifts in technology and processes are influencing the patterns of technical training, making them less predictable; they are compressing the training experience so that it is shorter but occurs more frequently. All this poses resource allocation problems for employers. However, if employers can recognize new training patterns for target groups and identify the most common providers of technical training, they can better determine how and when to establish effective training partnerships with external training suppliers.

Technical Professionals. Ninety-four percent of technical professionals require training to qualify for their positions. The requirements for preemployment training and credentials for this level of employee make four-year colleges and universities the most frequent suppliers of qualifying training for technical professionals; 63 percent of this group use four-year colleges and universities to qualify for their jobs. The second most common source of qualifying training for technical professionals is unstructured on-the-job training, which is used by 22 percent of technical professionals. These people rarely use formal employer-based training programs, two-year colleges and technical institutes, or the armed forces, to qualify for their positions.

Sixty percent of technical professionals require upgrading training to keep pace with rapid changes in their fields. Changing job requirements caused by advances in technology and the need to maintain professional certification or other credentials necessitate such training.

Unlike qualifying training, where one source of training is dominant, more sources are responsible for the skill upgrading of technical professionals. Formal employer-based training programs are the most common source of skill upgrading, providing training to 23 percent of all technical professionals. Unstructured on-the-job training programs provide 17 percent of this group with skill upgrading. Four-year colleges and universities provide 16 percent of the skill upgrading these employees need.

Technicians. Eighty-five percent of technicians require training to qualify for their positions. Because of certification or licensing demands, four-year colleges and universities are the most frequent training sources, being used 26 percent of the time. Unstructured on-the-job training programs are used nearly as frequently — 22 percent of the time. Qualifying training for technicians is rarely provided by postsecondary vocational, trade, and business schools; formal employer-based training programs; or the armed forces.

Fifty-two percent of technicians require upgrading training for the same reasons that technical professionals do: to maintain certification and to keep skills and knowledge current with changing technologies. Employer-based training programs are the most common source of skill upgrading for technicians and are used almost twice as frequently as all other sources combined. Seventeen percent of technicians receive upgrading training through unstructured on-the-job training programs and 16 percent receive it through formal employer-based training programs.

Skilled Trade (Blue-Collar) Workers. Sixty-six percent of all skilled trade workers require training to qualify for their positions. Because the content of the jobs of these workers is more practical and less theoretical than the jobs of technical professionals and technicians, skilled trade workers receive their training from different sources. These workers receive 39 percent of their qualifying training from unstructured on-the-job training programs. Skilled trade workers do not often use four-year colleges and universities for their qualifying training; only 2 percent of their qualifying training comes from those educational institutions. Similarly, other sources of technical training are rarely used by skilled trade workers to qualify for their jobs.

Skilled trade workers rely predominantly on employer-based training programs for their skill upgrading. Twenty percent of these employees use formal employer-based training programs, and 17 percent use unstructured on-the-job training for their skill upgrading.

Providers of Technical Training: A Brief Overview

All workers acquire their skills from a variety of training sources. The average worker uses an average of 1.3 sources of training to qualify for a job and to upgrade skills. Employers, educational institutions (including public and private two- and four-year schools), professional associations, original equipment manufacturers, other employer institutions, community-based organizations, vendors and consultants, and the armed forces are among the many providers that qualify entry-level workers for new technical jobs and upgrade the technical skills of employees currently in the work force.

Employer-based training is by far the most common source for technical workers. Formal and informal employer-based training is accessed for skills upgrading by about one-third of technical workers, twice the number that use schools. All technical workers receive nearly equal amounts of formal and informal employer-based training, with professionals receiving slightly more formal training and skilled trade workers receiving slightly more informal training.

Second only to employers, educational institutions are the most common provider of technical training. Virtually all technical workers who use schools for skill upgrading attend four-year colleges or two-year community colleges and technical institutes. Those who rely the most on school-based education are natural scientists and employees in health-related occupations

(88 to 96 percent), while between 50 and 75 percent of technicians and engineers rely on school-based education.

The remainder of this section describes employer-based training and educational and other institutions that provide training to technical workers and the technical populations they most often serve.

Employer-Provided Training

Employers are the largest provider of training for the technical work force. Overall, employer-provided training accounts for 43 percent of qualifying training and 38 percent of upgrading training for technical workers.

Although not the major source of qualifying training for technical professionals, formal and informal employer-provided training accounts for 37 percent of qualifying and 40 percent of upgrading training for this group.

Employer institutions play an even greater role in the training of technicians. Through both formal and informal programs, they provide qualifying training to 46 percent and upgrading training to 37 percent of this group.

Employers play their largest role in providing qualifying training to craft workers. Through their formal and informal training programs, employers provide qualifying training to 60 percent of craft workers. One way that employers provide training to skilled trade workers is through apprenticeship training programs. Since the establishment of a formalized registration system for apprenticeship training via the National Apprenticeship Act of 1937, more than 5 million youths have been trained through apprenticeships (AFL-CIO, 1988). An unknown number have been trained through nonregistered apprenticeship programs.

Compared to other industrialized nations, the United States trains the fewest number of youths through formalized and registered apprenticeship programs (Glover, 1986). As a result, many U.S. opinion leaders advocate that apprenticeship, with its combination of on-the-job training and off-the-job formal instruction, be preserved, strengthened, and extended to new occupations (AFL-CIO, 1988).

While employers continue to provide significant amounts of technical training with in-house resources, they are increasingly utilizing outside providers. This is especially apparent in the initial staffing of technical positions. More and more, employers are recruiting qualified workers prepared by educational institutions for entry-level technical positions rather than relying on on-the-job training or the variances of the internal labor market to ready workers for new positions. Once technical workers are on board, the challenge of upgrading skills is increasingly a shared one, with educational providers and employers joining together to keep workers' technical skills current.

External Training Providers

Training providers that are external to employer institutions have traditionally played a major role as a source of both qualifying and upgrading training for technical workers: they are responsible for 66 percent of qualifying training and 25 percent of skill upgrading for the technical work force. Moreover, employers are expected to turn increasingly to outside providers because they are a cost-effective means of providing training.

External training providers include educational institutions (four-year colleges and universities; community, technical, and junior colleges; and vocational, trade, and business schools), professional societies, original equipment manufacturers (OEMs), other employer institutions, community-based organizations, vendors and consultants, and the armed forces. Some of the providers may be accessed by individuals without the intervention of an employer institution; and those providers may operate independently of an employer. Workers can only access some providers, such as OEMs, through employer institutions. Other providers, especially educational institutions, may operate independently of or in cooperation with employer institutions.

The role of external providers is expected to grow over the next decade as employers struggle to deal with labor market changes. The current labor pool is marked by a shrinking number of eighteen- to twenty-four-year-olds and by millions of potential employees who lack technical and basic skills. Thirty percent of the growing labor pool is poor, unemployed, and unemployable (Butler, 1988). Without basic and technical skills training, these potential employees will be unable to supplement the current technical work force. External providers will be called upon to provide much of the basic training needed to ready these potential employees.

Educational Institutions. The United States supports 156 universities and 1,853 colleges with a combined enrollment of almost 8 million students. These institutions spend almost $80 billion annually, or roughly $13,000 per student. *Four-year colleges and universities* provide more qualifying and upgrading training for American workers than all other postsecondary educational institutions combined.

Often, technical training is offered through a school of technology within the university. In some cases, technical training is located in a division or department within the college of engineering or science.

The predominant focus of technical training programs in four-year colleges and universities is to provide qualifying training to technical professionals (including managers and professional specialists such as teachers, scientists, engineers, and doctors) and technicians (for fields such as manufacturing, construction, energy generation, communication, electronics, aviation, and medicine). Many institutions also have continuing education programs to provide advanced training and upgrading to these technical professionals and technicians. Four-year colleges and universities rarely train skilled trade workers, athough there are several programs that train instructors, administrators, researchers, and others who are responsible for organizing and operating high-quality programs for training skilled trade workers.

Just over 4 million technical workers received qualifying training from colleges and universities in 1985, and 1.2 million received upgrading. Technical occupations that are particularly reliant on colleges and universities for *qualifying* training include dentists (97 percent), biologists (94 percent), and physicians (93 percent). Technical occupations that are particularly reliant on colleges and universities for skill *upgrading* include speech therapists (48 percent), physicians (27 percent), and aerospace engineers (24 percent).

Community/junior colleges and technical institutes are part of the postsecondary occupational education system, which is the primary system for preparing high school graduates not going on to four-year colleges for nonsupervisory technical careers as technicians and skilled trade workers.

Students at community colleges and technical institutes tend to be older, poorer, and in greater need of basic skills training than are four-year college students. These two-year institutions are especially attractive to employed adults (a large percentage of the full- and part-time student body at these institutions is employed while attending classes) because of their accessibility and flexible class scheduling.

Historically, two-year community colleges and technical institutes have provided programs that prepare technician graduates for transfer to four-year colleges and universities or immediate entry into the labor force. In recent years, however, changes in technology, competition, and productivity have expanded this role, driving these institutions to expand their programs to address the training and retraining needs of displaced workers and other employees whose skills must be upgraded.

Community colleges and technical institutes are frequent providers of qualifying and upgrading training for technical workers, providing qualifying training to 1.6 million of them in 1985. In the same year, 760,000 technical workers received upgrading training from these sources.

Technical occupations that are particularly reliant on community colleges and technical institutes for *qualifying* training include inhalation therapists (46 percent), radiological technicians (39 percent), and dental hygienists (38 percent). Technical occupations that are particularly reliant on these institutions for skill *upgrading* include dental hygienists (13 percent), aerospace engineers (12 percent), and drafters (11 percent).

Vocational, trade, and business schools are also part of the postsecondary occupational education system and include both public and private institutions. Although these institutions tend to specialize in less technical fields than do two-year community colleges and technical institutes, they are also an important provider of training for skilled and semiskilled occupations. The traditional role of these institutions has been to prepare technicians and skilled trade workers for entry-level employment and apprenticeship programs or for more advanced postsecondary programs.

Vocational, trade, and business schools are noted for marketing their programs to adult learners. Private schools in this category, in particular, are noted for their short occupationally related programs and their flexible scheduling.

There is often a wide disparity in tuition and fees between public and private vocational, trade, and business schools. Also, because licensing requirements for these institutions vary among the states, there is a wide disparity in the quality of training they provide.

Vocational, trade, and business schools provided qualifying training for approximately 1.1 million technical workers and upgrading training for 300,000 technical workers in 1985. Technical occupations that are particularly reliant on *public* vocational, trade, and business schools for *qualifying* training include licensed practical nurses (25 percent), data-processing equipment repairers (12 percent), and heating and air-conditioning mechanics (9 percent). Technical workers who tend to receive their skill *upgrading* from these institutions include millwrights (6 percent) and dietitians (4 percent).

Technical occupations that are particularly reliant on *private* vocational, trade, and business schools for *qualifying* training include radiological technicians (19 percent), registered nurses (14 percent), and licensed practical nurses (12 percent). Technical workers who tend to receive their skill *upgrading* from these institutions include tool and die makers (6 percent) and health technicians (4 percent).

Military training accounts for the largest share of government training expenditures. In fiscal year 1989, $17.6 billion was appropriated to provide 249,168 man-years of training to people in all service branches (U.S. Department of Defense, 1988). Job-related technical training in the military includes the areas of electronics, computers, and aircraft engine repair.

In addition to the basic and specialized training offered by the military, each branch of service has cooperative arrangements with civilian schools to enable service personnel to earn high school diplomas or work toward college degrees. Among those occupations for which college credit can be earned are electronic technicians, aerospace engineers, and industrial equipment repairers. Several credit-by-examination and many correspondence programs are also offered. Finally, the U.S. Army, Navy, and Marine Corps have registered apprenticeship programs that allow enrollees to receive credit in civilian apprenticeship programs for their service experience.

Technical occupations that are particularly reliant on the armed forces for *qualifying* training include aircraft engine mechanics (45 percent), data-processing equipment repairers (22 percent), and repairers of electronic communication and industrial equipment (21 percent).

Many *professional societies* train technical workers (primarily technical professionals) through seminars, conferences, workshops, and trade shows. Many training programs are provided as part of a certification process. These societies also set the technical standards that industry uses to manufacture products.

Professional societies and associations reach thousands of technical professionals through their extensive publications on topics of technical interest. In addition, the staffs of professional associations are frequently very knowledgeable because they have the academic background and practical experience necessary to serve the needs of their profession and members. Therefore, they are usually good sources of current information about their field and its current needs and practices.

Seminars and workshops given by *consultants and vendors* are another means of educating and retraining technical workers (again, primarily technical professionals). Such seminars or workshops may be customized and presented at the employer's work site for several employees, or an employee may attend a public workshop offered by the vendor. Consultant and vendor programs range from focusing on highly technical subjects to providing skill upgrading in support areas such as computer language training and software engineering. The marketplace includes hundreds of consultants and vendors, including large national and international firms, small firms, and individuals.

Community-based organizations (CBOs) are usually created to serve a specific purpose (training, health maintenance, emergency assistance) or population (minorities, single mothers, children, youth). These organizations are nonprofit and often operate on shoestring budgets, supported privately or through federal, state, or local funding. Many CBOs are committed to developing a skilled work force, usually targeting their training services to those most in need: minorities, youth, and dislocated workers. The training that CBOs provide is almost always preemployment training; after the trainees have completed their training in a specific skill area, the organization helps them find jobs in the community. In some cases, however, training may be coordinated with a specific employer. In this case, trainees receive training in skills needed by the employer, and the employer selects new hires from among those who successfully complete the training. If funds and administrative regulations permit, some CBOs offer upgrading training to employers.

Employers may not link directly with a CBO. Often other providers, such as educational institutions, will subcontract to CBOs to fulfill a contract with an employer. This is done to make use of funds available for special populations that can be served by the educational institution's training program. Training provided by CBOs generally serves skilled trade workers, although technicians may also receive training from this source.

Relationships Between Employers and External Training Providers

To meet the challenge of training a technical work force that can cope with the demands of the new, technologically advanced workplace, employers and educators are building new — and more flexible — partnerships.

While employers are large suppliers of technical training, perhaps a more important role for them is to act as a bridge between their employees and external training providers. The relationships established between employers and external training providers spawn training opportunities in areas ranging from continuing engineering education to the remediation of basic skills for entry-level, nontechnical employees to prepare them to receive the training that will make them part of the technical work force.

By developing an understanding of the availability and services provided by external training providers, employers are able to make more informal training choices. They can take the initiative to build new relationships that will not only be more cost-effective for both the employer and provider but will have the end result of providing a renewable source of the skills and knowledge required for future employment in technical jobs.

Relationships between employers and external training providers can take many shapes and forms. Basically, however, such relationships fall into two categories: connections and linkages.

Connections are generally informal and largely advisory relationships whose primary function is information exchange. For employers this may mean advising a provider about labor market trends, industry skill needs, or the specifics of education or training programs that will prepare individuals to find jobs in the community. It may even mean an employer's encouraging an outside provider to train students in specific occupations by lending equipment for the training or consulting on curriculum design or delivery. For the provider, this kind of relationship hinges on providing feedback to the employer about provider capabilities in preparing the community's future work force or suggesting ways that employers can assist the provider in constructing strategies to meet industry needs.

Employers often view this kind of information exchange as a community service. Consequently, such connections do not necessarily result in the employer's hiring individuals trained by the provider. In fact, the main characteristics of connections are that (1) employers do not pay to have training set up or provided — the provider establishes the curriculum and enrolls students; (2) trainees are not current employees of the employer-adviser and may never be future employees, even if they are well trained, because the employer-adviser has not made a commitment to hire; and (3) employers sign no contracts and pay no money to support the training.

Some examples of connections are employer representation on provider advisory boards, exchange of technical training equipment between employer and provider, and lending of expertise (or even experts) to help identify industrial applications of technology and design curriculum for training in those applications.

Linkages, on the other hand, are formal, contractual relationships between employers and training providers whose function is to provide occupationally specific training or retraining for employed technical workers. Linkages are generally initiated by the employer to meet specific training needs. Employers pay external providers for training services and drive curriculum design and delivery methodology. Training is focused exclusively on the needs of the contracting employer.

Connections often lead to the establishment of linkages and vice versa. If, for example, the president of a local company serves on a community college advisory board, there is a connection between employer and provider. If, after attending several meetings, the company president concludes that the college can meet some of his or her firm's technical training needs, the president may offer to pay the college for establishing a specific technical training program for company employees. A linkage is established.

Conversely, when an employer purchases occupational training programs from a technical institute, it may lead to an advisory role or the employer may assist the institute's service to the community by donating equipment. Connections and linkages often foster each other and can be considered interdependent.

Following are descriptions and examples of effective connections and linkages between employers and external providers of training.

Connections

Connections are forged in many ways. Some of the most common are advisory committees, cooperative work experiences, personnel exchanges, curriculum sharing, continuing education, and networking.

Advisory Committees. Advisory committees are the most common form of connection between employers and educational institutions. They may also be the most formal of all connections, allowing a great deal of information to be shared between the two entities. This shared information helps educational institutions build a state-of-the-art curriculum and provides employers an opportunity to influence the preparation of technical workers from whose ranks they will choose future employees.

An advisory committee, composed of representatives from the local business community, is usually formed to provide advice to the leadership and administration of an educational institution and also to (1) help identify the employment and training needs in the community, (2) help develop and support the long-range goals of the educational institution, and (3) serve as a communication link between an educational institution and the private-sector community.

Technical advisory committees provide advice on course content, laboratory equipment and layout, and learning activities — they may even refer individuals for part-time teaching or consulting services. Committee members usually assist in evaluating students, placing graduates, and developing cooperative education openings.

Advisory committees and their members can be valuable resources and effective tools for improving the skills of the work force. However, the degree to which the committees are used varies from institution to institution, according to the scope of the assigned purpose and mission of each. The effectiveness of such committees depends on careful selection of members, clear delineation of committee responsibilities and roles, and attention to meeting schedules, arrangements, and communication. Educational institutions usually select industry representatives who have a sense of their firm's future technical training needs. Once on the committee, the representatives often participate long enough to gain a full appreciation of the institution; usually this means being involved in more than one event or cycle of the school's program. Close involvement of faculty with committee members is conducive to developing good working relationships and signals to both parties that the committee's role is important and members' advice will be taken seriously.

The CAD/CAM and Engineering Technology Program at Cuyahoga Community College in Cleveland, Ohio, operates fifty occupationally focused advisory panels each year. One such panel is the Engineering Technology Program Advisory Committee. Industries represented on the advisory panel include LTV, a major supplier of steel products to the automotive industry, with an annual revenue of $8 billion, and General Electric, a producer of major appliances and lighting products, with an annual revenue of $39 billion. The panel is composed of ten industry representatives, most of whom are either technical subject matter experts or training professionals.

The purpose of the panel is to inform the college about the preparation and retraining needs of technologists. Subject matter experts provide information about technical content and necessary equipment. Training specialists provide job analysis information and feedback about the knowledge, skills, and abilities that engineering technologists need to perform on the job. On the basis of panel input, the college establishes a generic technologist training curriculum applicable to all industries. The advisory panel reviews the course curriculum to determine whether any revisions are required. The committee meets twice a year to evaluate the program's success and recommend modifications. The companies that compose the advisory panel benefit from this relationship by being able to access an available and steady supply of well-trained technologists. The college benefits from an improved state-of-the-art curriculum.

Cooperative Work Experiences. Cooperative work experience programs (co-ops) place approximately 200,000 students per year in private-sector jobs while they are taking courses at educational institutions. Academic work and co-op experiences may take place simultaneously or may be alternated by academic semester. In co-ops, students receive an introduction to the realities of the workplace, get an opportunity to apply concepts and principles learned in the classroom, and earn wages that can help with educational expenses. Students return from co-op experiences with valuable insights and information that reflect current practices, problems, and levels of technology development in the private sector. Educators can take advantage of these insights to keep their academic programs current and to enhance and extend basic educational programs and tailor them to meet the needs of the private sector. Employers benefit from co-op programs by learning about potential employees and receiving students' workplace contributions, usually for less than full salary. Employers also have an opportunity to contribute important suggestions and information to help keep the school-based curriculum up-to-date and relevant.

Effective cooperative education programs entail careful development and planning to ensure that students experience realistic, educational work activities and that employers benefit from insights and skills that newcomers can bring to their businesses. It is also important that employers recognize the educational nature of the students' work experience and create opportunities to provide instructional input so that students gain as much as possible from their involvement.

Northeastern University (Boston, Mass.), well known for incorporating co-op programs into its curriculum, offers a five-year technical co-op program in which 2,000 students have participated. The first year of a student's education is spent on campus in a traditional academic setting. The remaining four years are spent alternating every six months between school and paid work experiences, usually with different employers for each cycle. Six months of continuous employment allows students to be involved in meaningful, long-term projects.

A faculty coordinator is responsible for placing students with area businesses. A student's immediate work supervisor at the employer site is responsible for structuring work and training experiences. The supervisor provides written feedback to the faculty coordinator about the student's work and academic progress. Corporations that have participated in the co-op program include General Electric, Honeywell, Digital Equipment Corporation, and IBM. IBM alone employs 240 co-op students each year.

Northeastern continually works to improve the experiences of its students and the university's connection to industry by observing and evaluating other co-op programs around the country.

Exchange of Personnel. Finding qualified technical instructors and keeping them abreast of rapidly changing technology is a major challenge for most schools. Educators may meet that challenge in two ways: by borrowing instructors from industry to teach students and by updating their faculty by sending them to work in industrial settings. Educational institutions often hire employees of local industries as part-time faculty to teach special one-time courses or to teach on a regular basis in the evening, on weekends, or during the summer. Using employees from industry, universities and colleges may tackle real industry problems on campus by funding research projects or ongoing programs that develop new technology.

Employers provide skill upgrading for technical faculty by offering programs that provide them with an opportunity to return to industry settings for extended periods of employment, often during the summer or other semester breaks, to update their knowledge and skills and apply them to new technological processes. Some companies also lend their technical employees to schools to conduct in-service training for their faculties.

Durham Technical Institute (Durham, North Carolina), a four-year technical college, keeps a planned microelectronic program as applicable to industry needs as possible. The school recruited a program instructor from industry to make site visits to employers with operational microelectronic programs to shape the course content and identify equipment requirements (Abram, Ashley, Faddis, and Wiant, 1982).

Cincinnati Milicron, one of the largest equipment manufacturers of industrial robots for factory automation, with annual revenues of $800 milion, provides training and technical assistance on robotics systems to the faculty of the Piedmont Technical College (Piedmont, South Carolina). This collaboration benefits the college by upgrading faculty and making them aware of Cincinnati Milicron's training needs. The collaboration benefits Cincinnati Milicron by ensuring a high-quality robotics training program and a steady supply of robotics technicians (Abram, Ashley, Faddis, and Wiant, 1982).

Sharing Curriculum. Postsecondary institutions and industry may share curriculum that one or the other has developed and that can be used in academic and industrial settings. Digital Equipment Corporation (DEC), a leading manufacturer of networked computer systems and associated communications equipment, with annual revenues of $9 billion, has supported a nationwide series of programs to train computer service technicians. Schools choosing to implement the program are given the curriculum and are free to adapt it to meet their specific needs. DEC also provides participating schools with equipment and trains the schools' instructors at its own training facilities (Abram, Ashley, Faddis, and Wiant, 1982).

Continuing Education. Continuing education is training for technical workers who want to expand their skills and knowledge beyond their current jobs. Continuing education can be distinguished from upgrading training in that upgrading provides technical workers with up-to-date information on technological advances on their *current* jobs, whereas continuing education reaches beyond job-related training and is focused on the *future.*

The relationship between employers and outside providers to provide continuing education is a nebulous one, requiring very little cooperation between the two entities. In fact, it is a relationship only to the extent that students in continuing education programs are associated with a particular employer. Continuing education is actually a connection between an employee and a training provider, with the employer playing a very minor role, perhaps as a coordinator or a conduit of information. The employer rarely has any input into the design or development of continuing education curricula.

Continuing education may consist of working toward a degree or a certificate or simply taking a course or series of courses relating to a particular field or discipline. Many schools offer continuing education students the option of taking a course for credit or for continuing education units (CEUs).

Continuing education is most often pursued by high-level technical workers, usually technical professionals, although technicians may also pursue continuing education. Technical professionals need to reach beyond their current jobs because they are on the cutting edge of technology — they are generally the employees who lead the organization into the future and create or expand the state of the art in their fields of expertise. Engineers are one group of technical professionals that regularly participates in continuing education. Rapid advancements in science and mathematics technology have increased this participation. Continuing education for engineers is most prevalent among manufacturing, electrical, and aeronautical engineers, although participation in continuing education is more heavily influenced by career level than by field or discipline (National Academy of Engineering, 1985). In addition to receiving continuing education in technical areas, senior-level engineers are much more likely to receive nontechnical training, particularly management training.

The pursuit of continuing education may be a broad requirement of employment. Scientists and engineers may be required to demonstrate their expertise by acquiring increasingly higher levels of education over a specified period of time. For example, they may be required to complete a master's degree within five years of employment or publish works in noted publications on a regular basis. Many employees not governed by such requirements often pursue continuing education for personal reasons such as self-improvement and career development. Employees may be motivated to pursue continuing education for pay increases or possible promotions. Generally, if the education pursued is job related (an ambiguous and often broadly defined term), the employer will pick up the tab, usually using an employee tuition assistance fund.

Four-year colleges and universities are the most common providers of continuing education because of the research opportunities and facilities available. However, two-year institutions and professional societies also provide continuing education courses. Employees usually attend courses at the educational institution on their own time, in the evening or on weekends, although some employers have brought college courses on-site

through arrangements with local universities; employees attend
on their own time but do not pay for the courses.

The University of Wisconsin, Madison, is an example
of a university that operates an extensive continuing education
program for engineers through its University Extension Office.
This program is unique in that it is staffed by a full-time faculty solely devoted to continuing education programs for engineers and offers a wide range of programs. Other universities
that have continuing education programs for engineers include
Purdue University, the University of Texas, Oklahoma State
University, Iowa State University, the University of Michigan,
the University of Illinois, the University of Arizona, and George
Washington University. All of these institutions have certain
characteristics in common:

- An availability of engineers as potential participants
- The support of local industry
- University support for continuing engineering education ac-
  tivities
- Support from the dean of the engineering school
- An active program director

Another method of providing continuing education to
high-level technical workers is for employers to allow these
employees to take sabbaticals. Sabbaticals are common in the
academic world and allow high-level technical personnel to pursue in-depth education and research full-time over an extended
period (a few months to a year or more).

In some cases, continuing education may occur on the
job. An employer may provide opportunities for employees to
broaden their knowledge in various areas by rotating them
among departments or units on *work exchange* assignments. For
example, the National Aeronautics and Space Administration,
which has numerous departments devoted to unique science
topics or problems, arranges to have a scientist from one area
work in another area for a specified period of time (a few months
to a year). Work exchange assignments are planned within the
headquarters of the agency responsible for broadening scientists' technical, management, and planning skills. These ex-

changes benefit the organization by ensuring an exchange of information for the benefit and enhancement of the total organization.

Networking. One of the most effective ways for individuals in the field of technical training and education to stay abreast of new technology is to talk with their peers. Numerous organizations and professional associations provide a forum for the exchange of information between professional vocational-technical educational personnel and employers. Associations geared toward educators are designed to improve program delivery, encourage scholarly attention in the field, and elevate the image of vocational-technical education. Interchanges among members of associations expose the members to new technological developments and state-of-the-art knowledge in many specialty areas. Even professionals outside these organizations have access to association information through journals, seminars, and conferences.

Students of vocational education also have numerous opportunities to interact with their peers and members of the business community. Organized vocational student organizations assist students in developing leadership and responsibility as well as technical skills. These organizations encourage learning and transition to the workplace by giving students the opportunity to function as junior members of trade, technical, and professional groups, as well as to practice and apply skills learned in the classroom and laboratory. Vocational student organizations operate on a not-for-profit basis, and their activities are supported primarily through student-paid dues to the local, state, and national organizations. Business, trade, and industry groups, technical and professional associations, foundations, and alumni of the vocational student organizations are accessed to provide students with information on the skills and knowledge they will need for a job in industry.

Linkages

Linkages can take a variety of shapes, largely depending upon employer need. They include customized training programs, state economic development programs, apprenticeship training programs, customer training providers, and training programs from other employers.

Customized Training Programs. By definition, linkages involve a buyer-seller relationship between an employer and an outside provider of training. Employers establish linkages for a specific purpose: to address an identified training need. A linkage may be a one-time relationship with a provider, or a provider may continue to provide training to an employer on an ongoing basis.

An employer may purchase a generic training program from a provider or work with a provider to develop a customized training program. Customized training programs are a desirable option for employers because they meet specific training needs. Potential providers of customized training are virtually limitless. Employers can link up with any number of organizations; a few of those most commonly used are illustrated below.

Some of the most innovative linkages that an employer can establish are with educational institutions. Each can benefit greatly from the other by making maximum use of the other's strengths. For example, employers have access to state-of-the-art technology, and educational institutions have the capacity and knowledge to conduct training on a large scale.

Industrial training programs offered to employer organizations through contract agreements are highly flexible and efficient and meet specific training needs. The most successful programs are aligned with organizational objectives and tailored to meet current business needs. Instruction is provided by regular or part-time faculty or by local experts and trainers recruited from other schools, industries, or the local training market (vendors and consultants). The curriculum is specifically developed for each program by personnel in the college training office and the client's organization. Needs assessment and job/task analysis techniques are applied in order to create a course that can deliver the particular competencies and skills the client requests. Technical, supervisory, and/or managerial training are offered as well as technical literacy and remedial courses.

Secondary vocational schools are not common providers of customized training to employers because the focus of these schools usually is not on the adult population. However, some, including the secondary vocational system in Ohio, have expanded their mission beyond the secondary level to address the needs of adults, especially those employed by local industries. Ohio has fifty regional secondary vocational schools called joint vocational schools (JVSs) to which students are sent from area feeder schools. In 1976, when these schools were established, Ohio made a commitment to train adults as well as senior high students in vocational skills. The Licking County JVS is one of the schools that has taken the commitment seriously. The school has been providing area businesses with customized training for more than ten years and has built a large vocational resource center (VRC) to meet the increasing demands for employer-based training.

The Utica, Ohio, plant of the Holophane Company, a producer of streetlights for highways, contracted with the VRC to train welders to weld light poles to their bases. Of eighty employees, fourteen welders needed to earn company certification. The ninety-six-hour customized program met from August 1987 to May 1988 in four-hour sessions twice each week. The classes were held on the company site in the evenings after the shift ended, and employees were paid for time spent in classes. The company paid for the program, although the VRC helped Holophane secure funds through the Ohio State Department of Development for companies that are expanding or upgrading. Holophane knew that the VRC would provide an excellent program; it had worked with VRC in the past on apprenticeship programs.

Declining enrollments in traditional two-year colleges and vocational and technical schools as the last of the baby-boom population has moved through the educational system have driven these schools to seek new clients aggressively. Offering customized training to business has proved to be financially rewarding to the schools as well as a valuable service to employers. Thousands of employed technical workers annually receive upgrading and retraining services through customized programs offered by these institutions.

Three-fourths of all two-year colleges offer customized or quick-start training programs. Most of these schools have an office responsible for developing contract-training services with local business and industry. Customized programs are usually directed by a coordinator who continues to maintain a long-term relationship with clients after the completion of a training program, thus ensuring close attention to special requirements and long-term quality.

In addition to training, two-year colleges offer other services to employers, including career counseling and remedial training to thousands of workers affected and/or displaced by changing technology.

Piedmont Technical College has long been involved in customized training. Monsanto Corporation, a large producer of chemical products, with an annual revenue of $6 billion, established a linkage with the college to provide a one-year customized maintenance technician program to fourteen employees. Monsanto agreed to hire all trainees who successfully completed the course. The company provided the school with job analysis information, which Piedmont used to develop the curriculum for the course. After its development, the curriculum was reviewed by Monsanto subject matter experts prior to being implemented. The company and the college worked together to develop a series of six criterion-referenced written and hands-on tests that were given to participants at the completion of the course.

Flexibility and coordination are key elements in the success of Piedmont's customized training programs. Flexibility at the college is marked by quick response to Monsanto's training needs and in course scheduling, program length, and faculty assignment. Coordination is marked by the extent to which the company and the college worked together to develop the program.

Crouse-Hinds Corporation, a divison of Cooper Industries, is a major manufacturer of electrical construction materials that has linked up with Onondaga Community College of Syracuse, New York, to assess the basic mathematical skills of its production employees in preparation for training in advanced manufacturing techniques. In cases where production workers' mathematical skills are deficient, the college counsels employees about the occupational necessity for skill upgrading and provides remedial mathematics training that precedes training in specific technical skills.

Four-year colleges and universities are not as aggressive in developing customized training linkages with employers as two-year colleges are. When the former do link up with employers to provide customized training, it is usually not in technical areas. Four-year colleges and universities are a widely used source for continuing education of technical professionals and technicians, however. Most universities do not have special offices that work specifically on customized training programs with industry. Usually these programs are coordinated by an employee in a continuing education department or another university office.

Employers can purchase prepackaged programs from *vendors and consultants* or can work with them to develop customized training programs. One advantage vendors and consultants offer over other providers is that they are extremely mobile and will usually come to the employer site regardless of location.

At American Telephone and Telegraph (AT&T), a major telecommunications employer, noted professors from leading technical universities, such as the Massachusetts Institute of Technology and the University of California, Berkeley, are contacted by the corporation to lead seminars on scientific topics at AT&T facilities. Before a contract is established between the consultant and AT&T, however, the consultant must demonstrate to the corporation's satisfaction an understanding of the subject content and an ability to teach adult learners. Potential consultants appear before a board of subject matter and instructional design experts to demonstrate their competency in these two areas. AT&T also reviews the course curriculum proposed by the consultant. After passing review, the consultant is certified as an AT&T science instructor.

Community-based organizations conduct customized training on a much smaller scale than other providers, generally because they do not have the funds to conduct this type of training on a large scale. Technical training can be very expensive, and

CBOs do not have the resources to purchase the specialized equipment that is often needed. One example of a CBO that does provide customized technical training is the nonprofit Opportunities Industrialization Center (OIC) in Philadelphia, Pennsylvania. The mission of the OIC is to provide a variety of services, including training, to special populations in the Philadelphia area.

Comcast Cablevision is a cable television franchisee that provides cable service to customers in the Philadelphia area. When the cable company first located in Philadelphia, it contracted with the OIC to provide preemployment training to thirty trainees, eleven of whom were hired by the company at the completion of the training program. Soon after start-up, Comcast began to grow very rapidly and, in 1988, needed to train seventy newly hired cable service technicians, cable installers, and line technicians. The OIC subcontracted with Temple University to provide the training but maintained an administrative role and monitored the program. The courses were provided on-site at Comcast and consisted of two classes lasting two weeks and two classes lasting four weeks. Because of the success of the program, Comcast plans to continue working with the OIC in the future.

State economic development programs have probably done more to foster linkages between employers and educational institutions than anything else. Most of the fifty states offer customized training as an incentive to employers considering relocating to the particular state or expanding their operations within the state. Educational institutions are being used more and more as a delivery system. These institutions, primarily community colleges and technical institutes, are targeted as deliverers because they are located throughout the state, and they already have the facilities and resources to offer the training.

Most economic development training programs are targeted at manufacturing industries and provide training in a variety of technical skills and occupations. Usually, the educational institution provides much more than just training programs; it links up with other organizations in the state when necessary to provide employee screening, recruiting, and hiring; customized training materials; job and task analyses; and much more.

Employers are equal partners in the development and delivery of the training programs. Representatives from the school and the company jointly plan a training development and implementation strategy.

In North Carolina, the Industrial Services Division (ISD) of the state's Board of Community Colleges assists the North Carolina Department of Commerce in luring prospective companies to the state by advertising the technical strengths of its community colleges. The board also gives technical assistance to community colleges by helping them design and implement quality training programs.

Similarly, networks of community colleges in South Carolina work as teams to transfer new technology to industry. For example, six community and technical colleges in the state share responsibility for different aspects of computer-aided design (CAD), such as sensors. The colleges optimize their resources by working as a team and having each college serve as a specialist for a particular area of CAD. Information is then shared among colleges in the network and used to help attract industry to the area.

Apprenticeship training programs require a three-way partnership between an employer, a labor union, and an educational institution (Warmbrod, Persavich, and L'Angelle, 1981). Contributions of the three entities vary and are subject to negotiation. For example, instructional content may be determined by the educational institution and the industry, whereas testing, interviewing, and candidate admission may be conducted according to government, company, and labor union guidelines. Instructors and facilities may be provided by the college and/or the employer, while master craft workers from the union guide the apprentice through various job experiences necessary for journeyman certification.

All three parties benefit from this collaboration. The union maintains control over admission to the program. Industry has a voice in determining what the apprentices are taught and receives workers who are academically better prepared than if they had not received formal, job-related training. The school improves its academic curricula, receives positive publicity, and gains assistance in fulfilling its mandate to serve the community. Two examples of how a local college and industry work jointly to provide apprenticeship training are given below.

The first six months of a four-year industry apprenticeship training program is provided by Cumberland County College in New Jersey. The twenty-six-week program incorporates an existing associate degree program at the college and an industry training program in engine lathe operation and associated machine shop practices. The apprentices receive one evening per week of related training from the college and forty hours of specialized technical training on-site from AT&T (Warmbrod, Persavich, and L'Angelle, 1981).

In 1981, Alabama Technical College in Gadsten, Alabama, teamed up with the local steel industry and the Bureau of Apprenticeship and Training at the U.S. Department of Labor. They developed a program to jointly train local apprentices in specific industrial-electrical occupations. The program included theory and practical laboratory experiences in the classroom and in an industrial setting. The program used a self-paced, individualized format (Warmbrod, Persavich, and L'Angelle, 1981).

Customer Training Providers. Employers can link up with their original equipment manufacturers to offer training to employees who are to use the new equipment. OEMs often offer customized training programs as a part of a package employers receive when they purchase equipment. OEMs also provide technical professionals from their customer organizations with information on the latest advancements in technical hardware. This permits technical professionals to make informed decisions about the purchase of equipment and the incorporation of new technology at their work sites. Among manufacturers that provide training to their customers are Cincinnati Milicron, a producer of machines, computer controls, and robotic systems, with annual revenues of $800 million; Westinghouse, a major appliances manufacturer, with annual revenues of $10 billion; and

Square D, a manufacturer of electronic control and industrial automation products, with annual revenues of $1 billion.

Training Programs from Other Employers. Employers can establish linkages with other employers to make maximum use of another's resources. Most employers are experts at what they do; other employers can tap these resources at a lower cost than developing the expertise themselves. United Technologies Corporation (UTC), a $17.2 billion high-technology products, systems design, and manufacturing company, is not in the commercial flight business but owns ten corporate jets and employs approximately forty pilots. Because of the enormous expense of obtaining the simulators necessary to conduct pilot training in-house, the only practical solution was to contract with an airline company that trains pilots to use the same kind of planes UTC owned. The company selected Trans World Airlines (TWA), a $4 billion commercial airline, to provide training to UTC pilots because of TWA's expertise and experience in providing pilot training. TWA trained UTC's new pilots and upgraded veteran pilots on a regular basis for ten years, until UTC sold its Boeing 727s in 1986 to purchase smaller aircraft.

Delivery of Technical Training Programs

It is important to recognize that relationships between employers and outside providers have improved efforts to provide technical training. However, other factors are also responsible for recent improvements in the provision of technical training. New, high-technology delivery methods—such as satellite networks and interactive video—make it faster and more efficient than ever before for employers and outside providers to work together to train technical employees.

Satellite Networks. The most significant of the high-tech delivery methods, satellite networks, are being used to aid employers in sharing programs and information with each other and allow universities to send programs easily and directly to employer sites. In fact, as a result of this technology, an entire university has been founded, a university that has no campus. Its programs are accessed by employees solely through satellite networks. The National Technological University (NTU) is a fully accredited, advanced degree awarding institution that delivers its programs by means of satellite delivery systems transmitted from various universities. NTU offers programs leading to a master of science degree in computer engineering, electrical engineering, computer science, engineering management, and manufacturing systems engineering. NTU has a board of directors composed of industry representatives who provide consultation on curriculum design and development.

The Association of Media-Based Continuing Engineering Education (AMCEE) also delivers educational courses to employer locations via satellite. AMCEE is a consortium of more than thirty universities committed to sharing information on continuing education for engineers, information that is delivered through the most advanced techniques. Ninety percent of all media-based graduate and continuing engineering education programs are represented by the AMCEE (National Academy of Engineering, 1985). AMCEE, like NTU, has an advisory panel composed of industry representatives who provide consultation on training needs.

A number of corporations have also joined together to transmit continuing education programs for engineers by satellite. These programs are usually developed internally or with the aid of universities and professional societies. They offer quality, in-depth courses that are on the cutting edge of technology. Course content focuses on current engineering job responsibilities.

Texas Instruments, a manufacturer of electronics products, including peripheral computer parts, with revenues exceeding $4 billion, and Dupont, a diversified chemical and energy company with profits exceeding $27 billion, are two companies that offer satellite courses to their employees and to employees of other organizations. Both offer day-long seminars on developments in electronic technology to other companies via satellite. Sharing courses through satellite networks makes technological advancements available to other organizations and encourages the spreading of costs of training and development among organizations.

Interactive Video Technology. Interactive video technology provides a training scenario that simulates a work environment and allows the trainee to be an active participant in the learning process. Although interactive video comes in various formats and levels of sophistication, most interactive video programs that are used by employers today are very sophisticated tape- or disc-based systems that merge video and computer technologies to produce a highly interactive system. The learner interacts with the video/computer, usually by means of a keyboard or touch-sensitive screen.

A typical interactive program combines graphics, text, and sound to provide an interesting and attention-grabbing experience that keeps the learner motivated. A unique feature of interactive training programs is that they allow the learner to access only those parts of a program that he or she needs. Random accessing allows the learner to jump ahead or repeat various sections as necessary rather than moving sequentially through the program.

Employers use interactive video training programs for several reasons:

- They are more cost efficient than more traditional learning systems.
- They are more time efficient than other learning systems.
- Training can be standardized and centrally controlled.
- Training can be delivered decentrally.
- The programs are competency based.
- They are self-paced.

Some form of interactive video technology is used for training or other purposes by 11.6 percent of organizations with fifty or more employees (Smith, 1987).

For interactive video programs to be effective, they must be carefully designed. These programs should be extremely creative in order to be memorable to the learner, they should motivate the learner to change behavior, and they should measure that change in behavior (Cohen, L'Allier, Stewart, 1987). Moreover, the organization of such programs should be clear; this is especially important because they are not linear. The pace should be quick enough to hold attention but not so fast as to confuse the learner, and the learner should have as much control over the program as possible (Smith, 1987). Finally, there should be some way for the employer to track the program user's progress.

A company that uses interactive video technology for training is Federal Express, a $188 million company that delivers packages overnight by air to locations throughout the United States. Domestic Ground Operations, one of three divisions of Federal Express, provides training through interactive video to maintenance and engineering personnel. Federal Express believes that interactive video is the most effective means for training this group. The programs are developed with a minimum use of text and maximum use of graphics, and employees move through the training program at their own pace. They work only on the skills they do not know and repeat exercises on those skills until they achieve the desired proficiency level. Federal Express can take the programs on-site, which minimizes the time that employees are off the job. The progress of the maintenance and engineering trainees is tracked by a Macintosh computer system that monitors the use of the program and the proficiency levels reached by the users.

CHAPTER 4

Best Practices
in Technical Training:
Centralized Systems

This chapter highlights three companies with centralized training systems. In each company, training is designed, developed, and delivered at the corporate level. The companies profiled are Carrier Corporation, Crouse-Hinds/Cooper Industries, and Niagara Mohawk Power Corporation.

Carrier Corporation

Carrier Corporation is a division of United Technologies, Inc., a major designer and manufacturer of high-technology products and systems serving the industrial, commercial, and defense-related aerospace markets. Other United Technologies divisions include Pratt and Whitney Engines, Otis Elevator, Sikorsky Helicopter, Norden Defense Systems, Hamilton Standard Controls, and United Technologies Automotive Systems. United Technologies employs approximately 190,000 people in 300 plants and a variety of sales offices located in fifty-seven countries. During 1987, the company realized a net income of $592 million on sales of $17.2 billion. This represented a significant increase over 1986, when net income was adversely affected by restructuring and employee severance write-off expenses.

Carrier Corporation is the world's leading manufacturer of heating, ventilation, and air-conditioning equipment. During

1987, it continued record sales for the fourth consecutive year by achieving sales of $3.2 billion (an increase of 14.3 percent over 1986 sales). Carrier's success is largely attributable to overseas expansion, a weaker dollar, increased sales volumes, and greater operating efficiencies.

Carrier and its subsidiaries employ 33,000 people in manufacturing plants and distribution and sales centers located throughout the world. The company's operations are organized under five major divisions: Purchasing, Centrifugal Refrigeration, Carlisle Compressor, Carrier Transicold, and Replacement Components. Carrier also has a research function that is structured under the Engineering/Research and Development group.

Three major efforts have contributed the most to Carrier's successful performance. First, the company has expanded its operations through sixty acquisitions and joint ventures in twenty-eight countries from the early through mid 1980s. As a result, the company has strengthened its distribution network, broadened its service base, and penetrated markets in countries otherwise closed to foreign manufacturers. Second, the company has continued to expand its highly successful replacement parts business (1987 net income increased by 65 percent), which was created in 1986 through the consolidation of its Carrier, Bryant, Day and Night, and Payne equipment components divisions. Third, operating costs have continued to decrease as a result of the company's five-year strategy (which was initiated in 1985) to reduce costs, streamline operations, and increase productivity.

Through its continued emphasis on research and development, Carrier plans to design and develop technically competitive and innovative products that offer greater efficiency and reliability and incorporate more precise electronic controls. This strategy is also supported by United Technologies through greater research and development funding.

Strategic Goals

During the past several years, United Technologies has examined all of its operations as part of an overall strategy to improve products and services and to increase its sales and earnings. United Technologies has grouped its operations into "core businesses" that reflect the greatest financial strength and potential. As a result of the corporation's operational assessment, numerous operations not fitting into a "core business" were divested, several other operations were realigned, overall employment was reduced, and overhead and material costs were decreased. Current and future strategies emphasize the expansion of United Technologies' "core businesses," becoming a more efficient and innovative manufacturer, and being more responsive to customers' needs.

As a division of United Technologies, Carrier completed an examination of its operations and as a result, reduced its employment, decreased its operating costs, and improved its productivity. Its expansion by acquisitions and joint ventures and its consolidation of replacement parts business also resulted from the operational assessment. Carrier's current and future strategy is to continue its expansion, increase operating efficiencies and reduce costs, and develop improved and technologically advanced products.

Training Structure

Organization. At Carrier, all phases of technical training are centralized. The technical training staff, which is located at the company's headquarters, designs, develops, conducts, and evaluates all technical training at Carrier. The Technical Training Department is organized under Industrial Relations (Personnel), which in turn reports to Manufacturing. The human resource function for hourly employees reports to the technical training. Technical training is structured under Manufacturing because 90 percent of the trainees are assigned to manufacturing operations.

Technical training works closely with plant management to evaluate current training and to determine additional training requirements. Through membership on the Corporate Planning Council with representatives from Carrier's five divisions and the Engineering/Research and Development group, the technical training manager is involved in discussions concerning new and existing equipment operations. This enables technical training personnel to plan and develop training courses well in advance of new equipment installation.

Through membership on the Corporate Training Council along with all other United Technologies training managers, the technical training manager can keep abreast of the latest training programs and techniques used at other United Technologies companies. This council meets twice a year.

Staffing. The Technical Training Department at Carrier employs six full-time and seven contract trainers. Full-time staff members have a background in the subject matter and are provided with instructor training if they have had no previous training in adult learning. The contract trainers are generally selected from local community colleges or vocational/technical schools. Carrier uses contract trainers as a cost-effective means of supplementing its full-time training staff.

Target Groups. Technical training at Carrier is limited to craft workers and first-line supervisors. Technical training's greatest emphasis and support in terms of management and funding is with craft workers involved in setup, operations, or maintenance. Course content includes mechanical, electrical, and electronics operations as well as safety and hazard communication. The second area of emphasis for technical training is with first-line supervisors employed in technical areas. They receive training in the same areas as craft workers do. Technical training for first-line supervisors is part of United Technologies' strategy for integrating management and technical skills.

Technical training at Carrier includes apprenticeship training, supervisory training, cross-training, retraining, and new technology training. It also includes remediation of basic skills on a continuing but voluntary basis.

The process for selecting training candidates commences with the development of a course schedule and entrance requirements. Both are listed in a training bulletin that is distributed throughout the targeted plants. Then the technical training staff accepts anyone meeting the entrance requirements, on a first come, first served basis. An exception to this procedure is made for newly promoted or transferred employees, who are automatically scheduled for training. Additionally, current employees are scheduled for skill updating whenever new equipment is installed or new technologies are implemented.

Linkages. The strongest linkage between technical training and other training programs is with Carrier's management development program for first-line supervisors. All courses for these supervisors are conducted by a team consisting of the technical training staff (for technical content) and management development trainers (for management skills). Other types of training are kept functionally separate from technical training.

The strongest links between technical training and other human resource functions are in the areas of wage administration and job evaluation for hourly employees. Both of these functions are organized under the Technical Training Department. Other less direct links between technical training and other human resource areas (affecting hourly employees) are also organized under the Technical Training Department.

Training Support of Strategic Goals

Technical training is actively involved in supporting Carrier's strategic goals. First, through participation on the Corporate Training Council, the technical training manager is kept advised about how other United Technologies Company training functions support their strategic goals. This interface with other United Technologies' training departments can be a source of new training concepts and techniques. Second, through membership on the Corporate Planning Council, the training manager is involved in discussions concerning the acquisition of new equipment. This enables the department to begin designing and developing supporting training packages immediately following procurement authorization and ultimately to provide the skills and knowledge Carrier's technical employees will need to handle new, more efficient equipment and technologies.

Crouse-Hinds/Cooper Industries

Crouse-Hinds is a division of Cooper Industries, a diversified, international manufacturing company doing business in three primary industry segments. Cooper Industries Electrical and Electronics Products segment, which includes Crouse-Hinds, Bussmann, Beldon Wire and Cable, McGraw-Edison Power Systems, Cooper Lighting, and other operations, manufactures equipment for primary and secondary transmission, distribution, and control of electricity and lighting for residential, industrial, and commercial users and wire and cable for electronic and consumer product markets. Cooper's Commercial and Industrial Products segment includes Cooper Air Tools, CooperTools, Kirsh, Wagner, and other operations, leading manufacturers and marketers of high-quality hand tools, industrial power tools, hardware, auto parts, drapery hardware, and window coverings used by consumers, craft workers, and industrial workers in construction, manufacturing, and do-it-yourself activities. Cooper's Compression and Drilling Products Division, which includes Ajax-Superior, Cooper-Bessemer Reciprocating, Cooper-Bessemer Rotating, Gardner-Denver Mining and Construction, and other operations, provides a broad line of machinery and aftermarket support services to oil and natural gas drilling, production, and transmission markets; industrial users; and mining and construction industries worldwide. Cooper Industries employs a total of approximately 45,000 people around the world.

As it did for many manufacturing companies, 1988 proved to be a challenging yet very rewarding year for Cooper Industries. The pressures it faced included steep rises in the cost of some raw materials and persistent volatility in the energy markets. The company's improved performance — on a per share basis, its second-best year ever — came as a result of strong demand for most of its products combined with benefits derived from its continued focus on increasing efficiency, maintaining and improving market position, and generating the levels of cash needed to fund acquisitions and capital programs.

As of 1988, Cooper was benefitting, along with the rest of the U.S. economy, from a sixth consecutive year of peacetime expansion — a postwar record. Improved demand from industrial, electronic, automotive, and some electrical markets plus the contributions of several complementary acquisitions boosted revenues almost 19 percent, from $3.6 billion in 1987 to $4.3 billion in 1988. Net income grew 29 percent, from $173.8 million to $224.4 million, reflecting not only higher revenues but also the benefits of manufacturing improvements and efficiencies gained from the integration of previous acquisitions. Fully diluted share earnings increased 27 percent, to $2.20 from $1.73 in 1987.

The continuing strength of the industrial sector contributed heavily to Cooper's gains. Industrial production and capacity utilization rose steadily during 1988, triggering additional spending for plant improvements and maintenance and raising sales of Cooper's products to its traditional markets. New construction spending, on the other hand, was mixed. Sluggish residential and commercial building was offset somewhat by stronger activity in industrial and highway construction.

Spending by utilities picked up in response to an increased demand for electricity, especially in rural areas, stimulating orders for Cooper's electrical protection products. Worldwide production of electronic equipment also continued on an upward trend that resumed in 1987.

Continued price volatility in world oil markets depressed petroleum equipment operations, but higher demand for natural gas and heightened activity in certain energy-related industries improved sales of Cooper's natural gas compression equipment. International markets in general were strong.

Crouse-Hinds, headquartered in Syracuse, New York, is the leading producer of explosion- and nonexplosion-proof fittings, enclosures, industrial lighting fixtures, plugs, and receptacles. Plant facilities are located in Texas, North Carolina, Illinois, Connecticut, and New York.

Although Crouse-Hinds's products are essentially medium to low tech, Cooper has invested heavily to modernize its plants into state-of-the-art facilities using high-tech manufacturing processes. This modernization has played a significant role in making Crouse-Hinds one of the most cost-efficient operations of its kind.

As a group, the operations in Cooper's Electrical and Electronic Products segment — its largest segment — once again recorded solid increases in both sales and operating earnings. It should be noted, however, that despite retaining a large degree of autonomy, Crouse-Hinds has been fully integrated into Cooper's electrical and electronics operations. Separate revenue and income figures for the company are therefore not available.

Strategic Goals

Cooper Industries is aggressively pursuing the goal of achieving leadership through its products, market position, financial performance, and return on investment, as well as by improving its manufacturing processes, developing and managing its human resources, and continuing its management philosophy of strength through value-added manufacturing. The company intends to become the most efficient supplier in each of its business areas while maintaining or achieving market leadership in each area.

The company is accomplishing this goal by pursuing three main strategies. First, Cooper is selectively broadening its product lines through acquisitions and new product development. As a part of this strategy, the company is acquiring complementary product lines and divesting itself of businesses that do not fit its long-term plans. Cooper is in a strong position for acquisitions and new product development programs because operating revenues and the divestiture of incompatible product lines generate the cash flow necessary for both acquisitions and programs to improve operating efficiency.

Integration of prior years' acquisitions continued throughout Cooper's operations during 1988. The consolidation and rationalization of all lighting operations, begun two years earlier, was completed successfully. Cooper now is one of the largest lighting fixture manufacturers in the world and has one of the broadest lines to offer customers.

A number of smaller, complementary product lines were acquired in 1988, along with two critical strategic acquisitions. The largest was RTE Corporation, a Wisconsin-based manufacturer of electrical distribution equipment. Consequently, what is now called Cooper Power Systems has emerged as the number-one player in distribution transformers and is a stronger competitor in the overall industry, with a wide range of products. The second strategic acquisition was Beswick, a manufacturer of fuses and related products in the United Kingdom. Beswick had provided an international presence that complements Cooper's very strong domestic market position.

Cooper's second strategy is to continue investing in manufacturing facilities and equipment to increase its operating efficiency. The company is continuing its investment in programs to improve the efficiency of its manufacturing facilities and to train its employees to solve customer problems in the most cost-effective way.

The third key strategy is to consolidate and streamline existing and newly acquired operations to reduce costs and improve customer service by taking advantage of common customers, distribution channels, and manufacturing processes. An example of this strategy can be seen in Cooper's consolidation of all lighting operations into a single group. This has enabled the company to integrate all administrative functions for all group members and to reorganize all manufacturing processes according to light source, with one or two factories producing specific lighting types within the group.

As a result of its strategies, Cooper Industries has developed a loyal, stable customer base by producing high-quality products that enjoy brand-name recognition. It holds leading or significant market positions in each of its key product areas. Cooper has also established itself firmly as a leader in relatively stable, lower-technology markets that are not subject to revolutionary change or obsolescence but can be expected to grow at approximately the same rate as the general economy and that are diverse enough to provide balance against fluctuations in the economy.

Crouse-Hinds's role in supporting Cooper's overall strategies lies in its ability to produce high-quality products that ensure its continued leadership within its market areas. Crouse-Hinds is continuing to renovate its facilities to incorporate state-of-the-art manufacturing processes, thus ensuring its high standing among its many customers.

Training Structure

Organization. Technical training at Crouse-Hinds is centralized, along with all other types of training. This centralization has been achieved by establishing a single training director who oversees all training activities from the company's headquarters in Syracuse. Located within Personnel, this centralized training function helps to achieve coordination among all training activities, facilitates better communication between training and the line functions, and enables the development of linkages between training and other human resource functions. Crouse-Hinds' training function reports both to company management and to the training function at Cooper's headquarters in Houston.

The training manager at Crouse-Hinds operates as a "one-person shop" but has developed a very close working relationship with company managers and employees. This network serves as the primary means for determining training needs and for gaining accurate feedback on training outcomes. Additionally, all performance appraisals contain a section on personal development and are routed through the training manager to help in identifying training needs.

Staffing. Since the training manager operates without a full-time staff, she or he has maximum flexibility to use outside resources as well as line personnel to meet the company's training needs. Much of the new equipment training that has become necessary as a result of plant modernization is conducted or provided by original equipment manufacturers (OEMs). This training is planned well in advance of equipment installation and is normally funded as a procurement cost. Additional support for training design and development is provided by local colleges and universities. All outside providers are prescreened, however, to ensure a thorough understanding of adult learning processes as well as the specific training need and desired outcomes.

Training is delivered through two sources. First, the outside providers responsible for development can also deliver the training. This delivery may be accomplished either on-site or at the provider's facility, depending on the type of training. For example, most OEM training takes place at the plant site. However, many of the college- and university-developed programs are delivered on campus on the employees' time but at company expense.

The second delivery source is through expert operations personnel who are selected to train their co-workers and then provided with a background in adult learning theory and train-the-trainer instruction.

Target Groups. The primary target groups for training at Crouse-Hinds include technical professionals, technicians, and craft workers. All target groups receive equal emphasis in training because both Crouse-Hinds's and Cooper's management firmly believe in developing their employees to their fullest potential.

Technical professionals at Crouse-Hinds consist mainly of engineers. They receive their training and development opportunities through OEM training, college and university programs, and courses provided in-house. Virtually all training provided to technical professionals is job related, and all is for skill and knowledge updating.

All craft workers are currently required to serve apprenticeships. However, as plant modernization continues, the craft worker and technician designations at Crouse-Hinds are gradually merging. All craft workers are currently required to pursue a two-year degree through a local college, following a curriculum that has been developed by the college to company specifications. The program includes courses intended to update the workers' skills and courses to help them develop professionally in nontechnical areas. The workers take the courses on their own time but at company expense. Upon completion of the program, all of the employees will be designated as technicians. Additional training is provided to both technicians and craft workers through OEMs or through other in-house programs using expert instructors.

In addition to the job- or task-specific training provided to each target group, Crouse-Hinds offers a full range of safety and hazard communication training to ensure full compliance with government regulation.

Linkages. Because training is centralized under one individual and located within Personnel, there is very close coordination among the various types of training provided to Crouse-Hinds employees. Aside from centralization, however, these linkages are attributable to three factors. First, staffing and employee development policies at the company encourage training all employees and filling vacancies from within. Second, the company's open training policy permits any employee to take any course offered through the company. Finally, the company is committed to maintaining strong communication links among all parts of the organization.

The principal links between technical training and other human resource functions exist through the appraisal and, more indirectly, through the compensation processes. A section of each employee's performance appraisal is devoted to professional development. By using the appraisal form together with employee interviews, the employee and his or her supervisor jointly identify skill or knowledge deficits and determine training needs. These appraisals are then reviewed by the training manager, who develops training plans to address the needs.

Technical training's link to compensation is due chiefly to the fact that Crouse-Hinds stresses that employee development is an individual benefit that will be provided and paid for by the company. Every employee is encouraged to participate in training, not only for general professional development but also to become more versatile and eligible for promotion to higher-paying positions.

One rather unusual but critical link to the human resource function is the company's outplacement program, which became necessary because of downsizing due to plant modernization and a market downturn. The program, which was introduced immediately upon notification of layoff, provided not only for job training to qualify workers for new positions with other companies but also provided counseling, typing support, telephone support, and a library facility for the employees. Through this program, 50 percent of the laid off employees were placed within eight to ten weeks and all were placed within six months after layoff.

Training Support of Strategic Goals

Management at both Crouse-Hinds and Cooper Industries believes that a key to corporate success is a well-trained work force. Training therefore plays a major role, not only by providing job training but also by providing additional professional development opportunities to all employees. Technical training directly supports the company's strategic goals by ensuring that all employees are provided with the best available job training as a means of assuring continued customer satisfaction with quality products and high name recognition.

Niagara Mohawk Power Corporation

Niagara Mohawk is an investor-owned utility that provides electricity and natural gas products and services to the largest customer service area in New York State. It supplies electricity to 1.46 million residential, commercial, and industrial customers within a 20,000-square-mile service area from Lake Erie to the New England border and from the Canadian border to Pennsylvania, and it provides natural gas to 450,000 customers in central, eastern, and northern New York. Within its service area, the company operates seventy-seven hydroelectric facilities, five fossil-fuel (coal, oil, and natural gas) plants, and two nuclear plants, as well as an integrated and interconnected (with other utilities) electricity transmission network. It also operates a 6,495-mile natural gas pipeline system. Moreover, Niagara Mohawk is involved in the growing business of providing electricity and gas transmission services to other utilities. Finally, under its diversified operations group, the company owns and operates the following businesses: Opinac Investments, Ltd., which is a Canadian-based investment and energy company as well as a utility; Hydra-Co, which builds and operates power production facilities; and NITECH, which markets advanced instrumentation systems to the utility industry.

In 1988, Niagara Mohawk posted operating revenues of $2.8 billion (up 6.9 percent from 1987), with net income of $482 million, an increase of 179.1 percent. The company employs 10,400 people throughout its operations.

In the past several years, the changing regulatory climate was a detriment to Niagara Mohawk's performance. In response to increasing public criticism over the funding of construction costs by utility customers, the New York Public Service Commission disallowed recovery of certain Nine Mile Two nuclear unit construction costs through the rate-setting process. Consequently, the company was required to write off the costs in 1987, which resulted in a significant and record loss. The company's high construction costs were in part attributable to the nationwide disfavor with nuclear energy, which caused delays during the planning, construction, testing, and start-up phases, as well as changes in federal and state regulations governing nuclear power generation. The latter factor caused numerous expensive modifications to be made during the actual construction period. Additionally, the New York Public Service Commission has continued to reduce the company's authorized rate of return on equity, which in turn has reduced net income and will reduce future profits.

Since 1987, Niagara Mohawk has undertaken an extensive cost reduction program to eliminate $100 million in costs. Costs are being or have been reduced through the elimination of 600 jobs, a reduction in officers' salaries, cutbacks in departmental budgets, and the postponement of projects not considered essential to daily operations. The company also increased its operating efficiency by reorganizing its structure along more functional lines.

In conjunction with the reorganization, the company created a new senior management team comprised of individuals who have both company experience and a fresh approach to business. The team is responsible for examining all facets of Niagara Mohawk's business to identify strengths and areas in which products and services can be expanded.

To further increase operating efficiencies and reduce costs, Niagara Mohawk has implemented a program to extend the operating life of its fossil-fuel power plants. Rather than replace aging plants with expensive new facilities, the company is emphasizing preventive maintenance and select refurbishment and modernization of existing plants as a more cost-effective alternative. An extensive test and monitoring system identifies which plants, systems, or components should be refurbished or should receive more intensive preventive maintenance.

In addition to reducing costs to improve its performance, Niagara Mohawk intends to capitalize on its basic strengths. Its primary strength is being a low-cost producer of an indispensable product — energy for homes and businesses. Its electric rates are generally the lowest in New York State and its gas rates are competitive with other regional suppliers. The company's plant and transmission facilities and employees are among the most productive in the entire industry. Its products and services are highly rated in terms of reliability and customer responsiveness. These strengths together with the rapid growth in its service area should help the company improve its performance.

The company's operating efficiency is also attributable to its mix of electric generating plants. Almost one-third of its electricity output is generated by hydroelectricity, which is the most economical electricity source. Of that, Niagara Mohawk produces 29 percent of its own power in this way, while 62 percent is purchased from other major utilities, and 9 percent is purchased from small independent hydroelectric plant operators. The backbone of the electric generating system is the company's coal-, oil-, and natural gas–fueled plants. Although these plants, on average, generate about one-third of the company's power output, this output varies in response to fluctuations in demand. With the company's program of upgrading rather than replacing existing plants and the low cost of fossil fuels, this power source has become relatively economic. Niagara Mohawk also operates two nuclear power units, which provide 14 percent of the company's output when in operation. While construction costs for nuclear plants have become prohibitive, their actual operating costs are relatively low and more predictable than fossil-fuel plants. The remainder of the company's power is purchased from other utilities.

Natural gas products and service businesses will also help the company improve its future performance. During the past several years, the price of gas has declined, making it more attractive for home and business use. With a continuing downward trend in prices and projected long-term availability, natural gas is expected to play a larger role in the company's financial performance.

Strategic Goals

Niagara Mohawk's primary objective is to become an innovative and responsive energy company that satisfies its customers' energy needs with a diversified line of quality- and price-competitive products and services. The company will continue to concentrate on its core businesses of electricity and gas products by striving to make them the preferred source for the largest possible number of energy users and uses.

To accomplish its objectives, Niagara Mohawk intends to defend aggressively its market share in key markets and applications, expand business opportunities with existing customers, and develop new markets for its existing products and services. The company will also explore and develop attractive opportunities in related business areas, such as advanced energy-related equipment and systems, value-added services, and power and gas transmission services for other utilities. It will continue to work with state and local agencies to promote the New York State area and to attract new businesses and revitalize existing ones.

To achieve its strategic goals and objectives, Niagara Mohawk intends to capitalize on its efficient and advanced infrastructure and its dedicated and well-trained work force (considered the company's most valuable resource). With its employees, the company will introduce new, innovative procedures and equipment, increase efficiency and productivity, and work with customers to improve service and identify new business opportunities.

Training Structure

Organization. Electricity and gas products and services are the core of Niagara Mohawk's business. Because the driving force is to make its electricity and gas products the preferred energy source for the largest possible number of energy users and uses, training and development is a major support service within the organization. Currently, more than 100 courses of instruction are available to employees. Many of these courses are mandated by federal and state regulations and collective bargaining agreements. The overall objective of the company's training programs is to increase productivity, promote human resource satisfaction and development, prepare employees for change, and ensure a safer work environment. Through the years, the company has depended on training to support new technologies, automation, scientific breakthroughs, more restrictive regulations, and a changing work force.

Created in 1974, Niagara Mohawk's Systems Training and Development Department controls and coordinates all training for all employees, with the exception of the nuclear division. The department is structured into seven activities — each headed by a training director — that represent the company's major training disciplines. The consumer services training activity provides technical and supervisory training and development to customer contact employees, including consumer relations and customer accounting personnel. The human resources development training activity provides training, education, and development courses to more than 2,000 of the company's managerial employees. The special programs training activity is responsible for the orientation of new employees and communication skills training for management employees. This group also provides all training programs, such as Operation New Employee (ONE), Litigation Avoidance, and Engineering Economics, that do not relate to specific activities. The service training activity provides technical training to employees assigned to the company's Service Department and also conducts service-related minitraining programs throughout the company. The operating training activity provides training programs to employees involved in the line, underground, gas, substations, welding, and transportation operations. The fossil generation training activity provides training support for the company's five major steam plants as well as materials management training for both fossil and nuclear personnel. Safety training was recently added as an activity under the umbrella of the Systems Training and Development Department and is responsible for all safety-related training programs, including Asbestos, Hazard Communications, and Work Area Protection.

The Systems Training and Development Department functions as a central activity, even though it has facilities in the following locations: Dunkirk steam plant, Albany steam plant, Dewey Avenue in Buffalo, technical training at Race Street in Buffalo, fossil generation training at the Oswego steam plant, technical training at Fulton Street in Syracuse, a training center at Towpath II in Syracuse, a training center at Seneca Street in Schenectady, and an administrative center at Towpath III in Syracuse, where the department's manager is located. The seven training activities are dispersed among the nine locations spanning 24,000 square miles of franchised territory, and in fact may share facilities with each other as well as with the company's operations activities. In the future, Niagara Mohawk intends to establish the Systems Training and Development Department within a centralized facility. There will, however, continue to be satellite training facilities in close proximity to the training target groups.

Because safety is a paramount concern and its operations and maintenance are so heavily regulated and closely monitored, all nuclear power operations are accomplished decentrally by a separate company training activity.

The amount of technical training accomplished by each of the seven activities varies, ranging from none for the human resource development and special programs activities to almost 100 percent for the consumer services activity. Basically, all of the training conducted by the nuclear training group is technical. Overall, approximately 5,222 employees are considered to be engaged in a technical occupation, and about 53 percent of the annual training budget is allocated to technical training. Technical training is considered a top priority of all training because it helps the company both maintain and update skill levels as mandated by regulatory agencies and collective bargaining agreements. It also contributes directly to company efforts to improve service quality and employee productivity.

Within the Systems Training and Development Department, training is generally designed and developed centrally by the appropriate training activity staff and presented either centrally at a group training facility or decentrally on-site, depending upon the training program, course, and location of trainees. In all cases, the staff works closely with the departments that will receive the training to ensure that all training requirements are met. The staff also assists individual operations areas in developing and conducting training courses that address issues unique to each area.

Staffing. Niagara Mohawk's Systems Training and Development Department currently has a staff of forty-four employees who are allocated as follows: The manager of system training and development, who reports to the vice-president of human resources, has one staff assistant (secretary); consumer services has a director and eight staff members (two of whom are CAI specialists); human resource development has one director and two staff members; the special programs activity has a director and three staff assistants; the service activity has two staff members; the operating activity has a director and seven staff instructors; the fossil generation activity has a director and ten instructors; and the safety activity has one director. Four represented employees provide steno/clerical support for the staff.

The Systems Training and Development Department has seven categories of staff positions, which are in hierarchical order: assistant instructors, who are virtually "in training" as trainers; instructors, who are responsible for stand-up instruction; associate training and development specialists, who are gradually introduced to program design and development in addition to their teaching assignments; training and development specialists, who are responsible for all new course design and development within their activity in addition to teaching; and senior training and development specialists, who now add consulting to their responsibilities beyond design and instruction. The other two staff categories are system training supervisor and system training director. Promotion within this progression is based on requirements for a B.S. degree plus zero years of experience at the lowest level to a B.S. plus twelve years of experience to qualify for "professional instructor status" at the senior level.

Niagara Mohawk uses a combination of the roles and competency levels listed in the American Society for Training and Development *Models for Excellence* and Kepner Trego as its primary models for determining its training staff job descriptions and for establishing selection criteria. In selecting new trainers, Niagara Mohawk first searches the applications to identify people with the required experience within a specific activity. The training director then narrows the field of applicants by means of weighted selection criteria (based on Kepner Trego). Finalists are often required to present exercises before a panel comprised of members of the training staff. Final selection is based on each applicant's technical expertise, communication skills, personality, and attitude.

Upon selection, the new trainer is immediately enrolled in an intensive train-the-trainer program that is conducted either in-house by the System Training and Development Department or outside the company in programs co-sponsored by Cornell University and the New York State Public Utilities Training Association under a contract agreement. Upon completing the program, the new trainer assumes the staff position for which he or she was recruited. Initially, the new instructor works with an experienced staff trainer who provides coaching throughout the first several training sessions. During that coaching period, the staff trainer continually evaluates the new instructor's performance to identify major strengths and areas needing improvement. The new instructor is then permitted to conduct training courses alone. After serving as an instructor for one year, which includes coaching time, the individual receives an annual evaluation. If the evaluation meets certain criteria, the trainer is then promoted to the next career step within the training progression.

Almost all of Niagara Mohawk's training is accomplished in-house by the company's training staff because this approach represents a significant cost savings. The company training staff is also considered to be more attuned than outside training providers to the company's operations, facilities and equipment, and requirements for training. The only exception to using company trainers occurs when new equipment is installed and the manufacturer provides the initial start-up training.

Target Groups. At Niagara Mohawk, managers, supervisors, technical professionals, technicians, and skilled trade workers receive technical training. Because most of the managers already have technical backgrounds, their training is usually limited to recurrent and "state-of-the-art" minicourses.

Because technical professionals, most of whom are engineers, and technicians also have technical backgrounds (they are hired for specific skills and experience), technical training is not provided as a routine or on a scheduled basis. Instead, training is provided in response to a "request for training," which is initiated by a field supervisor. The request describes the training requirement and includes a justification such as to teach a new skill, method, or technique; to broaden employee knowledge; to enhance self-development; to improve performance of an existing skill; to comply with company policy or regulations; to satisfy a job progression requirement; or to increase productivity. Once approved by the supervisor's senior officer, the request is forwarded to the manager of the Systems Training and Development Department, who then assigns the request to the appropriate group director. The director then meets with the original requester to determine the validity of the request, objectives of the proposed program, cost benefit of the program, and the best method for presenting the skills and knowledge required. Finally, the training group develops and delivers the program. In the past, there have been so many requests for training for these two target groups that the training department has had to refer the requests to senior-level management for prioritization.

Skilled trade workers receive the most technical training, which includes skills update, new technology, and personal development training. Much of the training provided to this target group is determined or mandated by collective bargaining agreements. However, additional training requirements are addressed through the same "request for training" procedure used for the technical professionals and technicians. The skilled trade workers actually receive certification in the subject matter following completion of each course and after having met the criteria and standards established for the course. Course participants are permitted to retake a course test only once to complete the course. If, after a second test, which must be taken within thirty days, an individual is unable to pass a course required for his or her job position, that individual must bid out of the job within ninety days.

Overall, the System Training and Development Department provides approximately 100 training programs and courses, which range from the nontechnical (such as Leadership Training, Communications Skills, Supervisory Skills, and Service Representative Training for Gas and Electric) to the technical (such as Steam Plant Operator Training, Boiler/Furnace Analysis, Chemistry Technician Progression, Electrician Progression, and Gas Mechanic Progression). Course offerings are about evenly split between operations and maintenance training and customer service and communications training. Training methods consist of classroom instruction and the use of self-paced manuals, videos, and computer-assisted instruction.

As part of Niagara Mohawk's Corporate Austerity Program, the training department has been required to review its programs and assign priorities on the basis of cost/benefit and regulatory or company requirement. Contrary to the mistaken belief that when budgets are cut "training is the first to go," a critical review of the entire training operation by senior management resulted in the reinstatement of pending expense reductions and in the *addition* of staff. The training department continually evaluates all programs to verify that each has a definite benefit to the company's operations. The evaluation consists of student and supervisor feedback after course completion and a reverse review six months after course completion by the trainee, subordinates, supervisors, and peer groups. On the basis of this evaluation, courses are continually updated or, if warranted, discontinued.

Linkages. Because all types of training (except nuclear power training) are controlled and managed by the Niagara

Mohawk System Training and Development Department, they tend to be closely linked. And because each of the department's seven activities presents some technical training, it is not uncommon for technical training to be presented in combination with some other type of training. For example, when the consumer services activity trains the company's customer contract employees who read electric or gas meters, it also includes technical training concerning the portable electronic meter-reading devices. Conversely, all four training groups are now including both supervisory and communications skills training with their technical training in response to a new company emphasis on these skills.

While there is no direct link between technical training and other human resource functions, training does provide several curricula that support career advancement and enhance the employees' performance levels. Training curricula for electricians, chemistry technicians, mechanics, and gas mechanics offer a series of courses that progress from a basic understanding of the subject area to a more advanced concentration in specific areas. An employee's compensation level and promotability are linked to proficiency and knowledge levels gained from training.

Training Support of Strategic Goals

Technical training at Niagara Mohawk directly supports the company's strategic goals. Training helps reduce operating costs by providing the skills and knowledge employees need to function more efficiently and productively. With its new emphasis on supervisory and communications skills training, the training department helps to foster greater cooperation and teamwork among the company's employees. Training continually promotes customer relations in a variety of courses that can be presented alone or as a supplement to other training. It also supports the company's existing operations and equipment and newly implemented technologies by providing update training as well as new technology training. This is especially critical as Niagara Mohawk continues to upgrade its electricity generation and transmission network both to improve product and service quality and to expand into new services and service areas. Finally, training supports the company in complying with a variety of federal and state regulations that cover not only electrical power generation and transmission (as well as natural gas transmission) but also issues such as safety and plant emissions.

A more indirect way in which technical training supports the company's strategic goals is in its efforts to recover some training costs (as part of the company's austerity program) through packaging selected courses for sale outside Niagara Mohawk. For example, it is currently marketing nationally an interactive video program that trains meter readers to use new portable meter-reading devices and is contracting technical training for the Fort Drum military base personnel in Watertown, New York.

Having gained the support of "top management" and the cooperation of the union through the delivery of quality programs while at the same time developing a highly professional staff, technical training has one remaining long-range goal: a permanent centralized training facility.

CHAPTER 5

Best Practices in Technical Training: Decentralized Systems

This chapter highlights three companies with decentralized training systems. The majority of the training at Alcoa is decentralized, with each location responsible for its own technical training. Federal Express has no corporate-level training function; each of its three divisions is responsible for its own training. Ford has a central training department, but the majority of its training is designed, developed, and delivered by each of its departments and divisions.

Alcoa

Alcoa is the world's largest aluminum company, as measured by total assets, revenue, and aluminum shipments. The company's primary business of fabricating aluminum products is supported by a variety of operations involving the aluminum production process. These operations include mining bauxite, refining bauxite into alumina, smelting the alumina into primary aluminum, and fabricating the metal into a variety of aluminum alloy products. These products are used in numerous packaging, transportation, building, defense, and industrial applications. The company also supplies aluminum ingot and alumina to users outside the Alcoa system. In addition, Alcoa is the world's largest recycler of used aluminum beverage cans.

Other products produced by Alcoa include various chemicals and engineered products made from alumina, aluminum, and other materials. Alcoa also generates electricity for some of its smelters and operates trucking and ocean shipping lines to transport Alcoa products and raw materials. As a technological leader in the industry, Alcoa operates the world's largest light metals research organization.

In 1988, Alcoa earned $861 million on sales of $9.8 billion. These earnings were generated primarily from the sale of 2.5 million metric tons of aluminum products. By the end of 1988, Alcoa's assets were valued at $10.5 billion. Alcoa employs 59,000 people (34,000 in the United States) at 140 operating and sales locations in eighteen countries in North and South America, Australia, Europe, Asia, and Africa.

Contributing to Alcoa's strong performance in 1988 were an excellent economic environment and the strongest market for aluminum since the mid-1970s. Alcoa celebrated its centennial in 1988 and enjoyed the distinction of remaining at the top of its industry for the entire 100-year period.

During 1988, Alcoa took several actions to further improve its performance. First, the company sold a number of low-return businesses and select surplus assets, generating $186 million in cash. Second, the company reduced long-term debt by $941 million (which represented 36 percent of total long-term debt). Third, consistent with Alcoa's increasing emphasis on quality, a new Quality Department was established at the vice president level. Fourth, the company continued its program aimed at improved safety performance, with a decrease of 20 percent in the number of serious injuries companywide. As a result, Alcoa continued to lead the aluminum industry in safety performance. Fifth, Alcoa implemented a new profit-sharing program for hourly and salaried employees at the company's U.S. aluminum operations. This new program enables participants to share in the profits upon the attainment of a specified threshold. Sixth, the company established a new management incentive program that links individual and group rewards to targeted profit objectives. Finally, the company reached new labor agreements with major unions covering 15,000 employees located in fourteen U.S. plants. These agreements extend into mid-1992. Although most of the foregoing actions were intended to improve Alcoa's performance over the long term, many of them resulted in immediate operational and financial benefits.

The company's accomplishments in 1988 were a continuation of the major effort made by Alcoa to strengthen its performance in aluminum and engineered materials through operational restructuring and streamlining. Since 1985, this restructuring and streamlining has taken several courses. First, Alcoa invested an average of $860 million annually, from 1985 to the present, in new and replacement equipment and facilities that are more productive and that, in some cases, produce new, high-technology products. In fact, one new facility that opened in 1988 is a high-technology mill (the first of its kind in the world) that produces aluminum sheet for beverage cans. Another new facility, scheduled to open in 1989, will produce electronic ceramics for the computer industry. Second, the company closed or sold several less efficient alumninum plants. Third, the company wrote off $231 million in assets that did not meet the company's performance objectives. Fourth, Alcoa sold assets valued at $47 million, which in turn provided funds for higher-priority projects. Fifth, Alcoa continued to decrease its annual interest costs by reducing its long-term debt.

Alcoa recognizes that the current favorable economic environment, which has improved aluminum markets for the past several years, is temporary and that eventually volume demand and prices will weaken. At the same time, the entire aluminum industry has experienced increased international competitive pressure. The actions taken during the past several years to improve the operations of its core businesses, expand its current product lines, and develop and introduce new products represent Alcoa's strategy to surmount these economic factors.

Strategic Goals

To continue its successful performance and to overcome potential adverse economic conditions, Alcoa is pursuing three major operational strategies. First, the company intends to expand the use to aluminum worldwide, especially in potential high-growth markets located in Europe, Asia, South America, and the Pacific Rim. It plans to aggressively pursue opportunities in developing countries, where per capita consumption of aluminum products is expected to increase as living standards increase. Second, Alcoa intends to become the supplier of choice for aluminum and alumina products. The company will accomplish this objective by anticipating both the present and future needs of its customers and by producing high-quality aluminum products that meet its customers' exacting demands. The company also intends to adopt a more "partnership-type" relationship with its customers. Third, Alcoa plans to become a world leader in quality. The company recognizes that to succeed in the increasingly competitive, global marketplace, it must attain a high degree of quality not only in its products but in everything it does. Alcoa's new corporate organization is a reflection of this commitment to quality.

In addition to these strategic goals, Alcoa is also pursuing the financial goal of a 15 percent return on equity. The company's restructuring and streamlining efforts as well as its three operational goals are intended to help Alcoa achieve this financial objective.

Training Structure

The majority of technical training at Alcoa is decentralized within several areas of the corporation. Essentially, each location is responsible for its own technical training function, which is structured under that location's organization. There is no formal organizational link among the various technical training functions. This review examines technical training at two locations: Alcoa Laboratories and Tennessee Operations.

Organization. Alcoa Laboratories is the research arm of the corporation. Its responsibility is to meet the needs of tomorrow's markets for commercial and military aerospace, packaging, biotechnology, electronic packaging, high-temperature processing, and transportatioin by providing unparalleled technical excellence in aluminum, engineered materials, and related competitive technologies. As a result, much of the laboratories' research involves aluminum and aluminum alloys, ceramics, polymers, and composites. Alcoa Laboratories is composed of a primary facility (Alcoa Technical Center) and a smaller research facility (Alcoa Research Laboratory), both located near Alcoa's corporate headquarters in Pittsburgh, Pennsylvania. Additional smaller research facilities are located at other sites throughout the United States. This review focuses primarily on the technical training accomplished at Alcoa Technical Center, which employs 1,351 people.

The technical training function at Alcoa Laboratories is responsible for the design, development, delivery, and evaluation of training for all employees of the labs. Although not a formal responsibility of the laboratories' training organization, some training is also provided, upon request, to employees from other Alcoa locations and subsidiaries. Technical training is structured under the Education and Training Department, which is part of Alcoa Laboratories' Human Resources Department. The training staff is located at Alcoa Technical Center (ATC), while the primary training facility is housed at another location halfway between the center and the corporate headquarters building.

The corporation's plant in Alcoa, Tennessee (near Knoxville), produces both primary products and fabricated aluminum sheet. The operation includes aluminum smelting, aluminum can recycling, ingot production, hot rolling, cold rolling, sheet finishing, and packaging. Approximately 3,200 people are employed in two plant locations, and the major product is high-quality aluminum sheet used in the manufacture of aluminum beverage cans. The operation is currently involved in an extensive equipment modernization program to bring automated equipment that will provide the high-quality aluminum products demanded by the marketplace. The eight-year modernization will involve an investment of approximately $500 million, with $150 million funding the installation of a state-of-the-art continuous cold-rolling mill.

During the entire modernization period, technical training will play a critical role in supporting the transition from the older production equipment and processes to the new automated production equipment and techniques. A training program was designed for each of the major pieces of new equipment and included basic process considerations, basic equipment operation, and the maintenance aspects of the equipment. With the new cold-rolling mill as the centerpiece of the modernization effort, special attention was given to both the selection and training of the employees involved. The training department assisted in the design and implementation of the employee selection system and then designed a detailed training plan for both the classroom and hands-on portions of the training. Employees were brought into the new cold mill department nine months ahead of the projected mill start-up. They were given intensive training in process, operation, and maintenance of the new equipment, along with team-building training, and then heavily involved in the six-month commissioning of the new mill. Even though Alcoa spent well over $3 million to train the employees of the automated cold-rolling mill, the successful commissioning and rapid production "learning curve" have more than justified the training expense. Moreover, that same initial intensive training program serves as a prototype for much of the technical training accomplished at the plant today.

The technical training functions at the Alcoa, Tennessee, plant are part of a central training department that provides needs assessment, instructional design, program development and delivery, and evaluation of training at the two plant sites. Upon request, this training department also provides support to employees from other Alcoa plants. An informal relationship among the training functions at the various Alcoa locations allows the exchange of training data and ideas. There is also a formal annual meeting among the domestic locations to discuss a variety of common technical training issues.

At the Tennessee location, the training department reports through the personnel manager to the operations manager. The operations manager in turn reports to a corporate manufacturing manager. The training staff and facilities, including offices, classrooms, plant training lab, video studio, and computer training facilities, are located in a training center near the two Tennessee plant sites.

Staffing. The training staff at Alcoa Laboratories consists of nine full-time training professionals, of whom seven are Alcoa employees and two are full-time consultants. One to three part-time employees supplement the full-time staff. Staff members are selected for their backgrounds in adult learning with specialties in instructional design and educational delivery. Approximately half of the staff is involved in the design and development of training courseware, while other members are involved in the management of the facilities and technologies associated with the large number of media-based courses.

Course development is generally accomplished by a team consisting of a staff instructional design specialist, an expert on the subject from Alcoa Laboratories, and an outside training contractor with subject matter expertise. The staff trainer and the subject matter expert initiate the training development process by reviewing a training problem or opportunity and establishing a list of training objectives. An outside trainer is then hired to design, develop, and teach the training package under the direction and guidance of the staff trainer and subject matter expert. Training staff members basically serve as project managers over the contracted trainers because this arrangement is considered more cost-effective (by enabling more course development per staff member). Although most of the courses are also delivered by contract trainers, each staff trainer is required to deliver one course per year to maintain a competency in training delivery.

At Alcoa Laboratories, training direction and curricula are determined by twenty curriculum committees, representing the various labs' technologies (such as advanced manufacturing technologies, heat transfer, chemistry, and computers) and other training requirements (such as professional development and administrative and clerical skills). The committees, which include members from all employment levels, meet with the training staff on a regular basis to identify course and curriculum requirements as well as the future training direction for their respective areas. The training staff then meets biweekly with other department members to provide updates on programs under development, to problem solve, and to plan direction and activities.

The technical training staff at the Tennessee plant consists of six salaried employees and ten hourly employees. This group is supplemented by a variable size group of contract employees, who are typically employed through a local two-year state technical school. The majority of the training is designed by teams consisting of instructional designers and plant subject matter experts. Much of the technical training is then delivered by a subject matter expert.

The instructional designers are selected for their design skills and ability to express the instructional needs in writing. They also must have the ability to obtain information from the plant subject matter experts. All instructional designers are given in-house training in instructional design to ensure a consistent methodology. Both in-house and contract employees are used in the instructional design area.

All potential instructors are selected for their subject matter expertise and their ability to convey skills and knowledge to trainees in an effective manner. Each instructor must undergo a testing and interviewing process prior to selection. Once selected, each instructor attends a five-day train-the-trainer course, with additional training as required. To keep up-to-date in their subject areas, all instructors attend refresher and new technology training in their respective fields. This update training can last from several days to several weeks each year.

On some new equipment, the equipment vendor will present the initial training to the plant area personnel with technical instructors in attendance. Generally, the technical instructors will then take responsibility for the subsequent training sessions as well as the maintenance of the particular training program.

Target Groups. Technical training at Alcoa Laboratories is primarily provided to managers, technical professionals (engineers and scientists), and laboratory technicians located at the facility. Upon request, training may also be provided to engineers from other Alcoa locations on a space-available basis. Because of concerns that rapidly changing technologies are accelerating career obsolescence, technical professionals receive much of the training emphasis. Generally, the training subject matter involves the twenty technologies and other training requirements of the curriculum committees. Additionally, it includes safety, hazard communication, and quality, which have become increasing concerns of the corporation. During 1988, Alcoa Laboratories' training function offered 104 instructor-led courses and 95 noncredit courses (by satellite).

Alcoa Laboratories' training function also operates two resource centers that together offer 325 media-based courses (such as Industrial Operations, Computer Science, Safety, and Personnel and Career Development) for independent study. Although primarily intended for Alcoa Laboratories personnel, the courses, most of which are video based, have also been made available to other Alcoa employees. The courseware is usually purchased off-the-shelf, although the training staff has developed several courses in-house. In fact, two staff-developed courses have become eligible for university credit.

Eighteen graduate-level and two undergraduate-level degree programs are offered to employees (primarily engineers, scientists, and technicians) of the laboratories. Alcoa Technical Center also has access to nine channels of programming for broadcast of courses from universities linked by satellite.

The responsibility for professional development at Alcoa Laboratories lies with the individual employee. Each employee is encouraged (but not required) to complete between 40 and 100 hours of training per year. With Alcoa's increased emphasis on safety and quality, all employees are also receiving more training in these two areas. A computerized training management system located at Alcoa Laboratories tracks training progress by course, individual, supervisor, or division.

At the Alcoa, Tennessee, plant, the primary audiences for the technical training developed by the training department are the hourly equipment operators, skilled hourly craftworkers, first-level supervisors, and maintenance technicians. In addition, some professional technical employees and higher-level supervisors receive technical training courses at the training center. The training department is responsible for administering an apprenticeship program for each of the location's five apprenticing crafts (electrician, machinist, mechanic, construction specialist, and truck repair mechanic). Each apprenticeship is a 6,000-hour program, usually completed over three years and consisting of approximately 4,800 hours of on-the-job training and 1,200 hours of related classroom and laboratory instruction. The training department schedules and monitors the entire apprenticeship program and maintains the proper records. All of the apprenticeship programs are recognized by the U.S. Department of Labor's Bureau of Apprenticeship Training.

Because of the automated and complex nature of the modernized plant and continuous drive for quality and safety, heavy emphasis is also placed on upgrade training for the plant operators, craft journeymen, and their first-level supervisors. The training subject matter generally addresses either a specific training problem or a new process or piece of equipment. Requests for training are usually initiated by the various plant departments (operating, maintenance, or staff groups); occasionally, however, the training department identifies a particular training requirement. Currently, over 200 different in-house technical courses are offered by the training department. Each year new courses are designed and developed with an emphasis on retrievability for future groups. Most of the training is currently delivered in a classroom or laboratory instruction mode. The training is supplemented with video, interactive computer-based training, equipment simulation, and on-the-job training. Another current trend is to develop a variety of self-paced technical instruction materials to meet the needs of differing learning rates and variable class sizes.

Training is also provided for the plant's technical professionals and technicians. This training is generally limited to more advanced technical issues, new equipment operation, and specific concerns (such as quality and safety) of plant management. It has also proven very beneficial to cover many of the practical plant technical issues for new engineers. In addition, the Tennessee plant is working with the Alcoa Laboratories training group to develop a satellite education option for the local plant's professional employees.

Consistent with the interplant cooperation and exchange of ideas and data, the Alcoa, Tennessee, plant provides informal training support (on a reimbursement basis) to other plants. The support varies from the training of other plants' instructors to the copying of technical course outlines. Training staff members at the Tennessee plant may conduct training at another Alcoa location or provide consulting assistance.

The training function at the Tennessee plant is overseen by an operations training committee consisting of the training director, the operations manager, the two plant production and maintenance managers, the engineering manager, the personnel manager, and the financial manager. This group serves as a strategic direction-setting group for the training department and also helps in assigning project priorities.

Linkages. Linkages between technical and other training programs are the most clearly defined at Alcoa Laboratories, where individual learning plans are developed for all employees. Since employees at Alcoa Laboratories are responsible for their own professional and career development, the individualized plans serve as a guide and list the technical and nontechnical training required for each employee to achieve his or her professional and career goals.

At the Alcoa, Tennessee, plant, the employee performance appraisal process helps link job performance to specific training needs for salaried employees. In some plant areas, individual learning contracts are now being used as guidelines for future training requirements. For hourly production and maintenance workers, the job classification descriptions and the new equipment help drive the training development process.

One of the strongest links between technical training and other human resource functions can be seen in the craft apprenticeship program. In this program, task analysis becomes the basis for job descriptions, selection systems, compensation, and training requirements. Training is also linked directly to labor relations because the basic mechanisms of the apprenticeship program are defined in the plant's negotiated labor agreement.

Training Support of Strategic Goals

Alcoa intends to maintain its leadership role in the aluminum industry and to expand its position in the engineered materials business. To achieve this, Alcoa must develop new products and manufacturing technologies, upgrade existing facilities, and expand into new markets. The company also intends to aggressively incorporate quality in all of its operations and products and to become the aluminum industry's premier supplier. Alcoa management is convinced that only through highly dedicated, competent, and skilled employees can the company achieve its goals and maintain its industry leadership during its second 100 years. Technical training supports these strategic goals by providing its employees with the skills and knowledge necessary to operate high-technology plants and equipment that produce increasingly sophisticated products. Technical training also continues to update employee skills as new advanced equipment and products are introduced.

Federal Express Corporation

Federal Express Corporation was the first company to engage in the overnight delivery of packages by air in the United States. Federal Express pioneered in processing packages through a single hub facility for overnight delivery to any location in the country. Currently, the company remains the leader and one of the largest in the industry, with 241 aircraft, 21,000 delivery vehicles, more than 1,200 Federal Express offices worldwide (including 400 business service centers and 275 drivethrough kiosks in the United States), and more than 60,000 employees. The company operates package sorting centers at its superhub in Memphis and in regional hubs located in Oakland, Newark, and Brussels. In addition to its U.S. operations, the company also provides international service to more than 100 countries either through subsidiaries or independent contractors. During fiscal year 1988, the company processed 226 million documents and packages, yielding $3.883 billion in revenue (up 22.2 percent from 1987 revenue) and $187.716 million in net income (up 386.3 percent).

Federal Express attributes much of its success to its conscientious, efficient, and quality- and service-oriented work force. The company believes that a well-trained and highly motivated work force is crucial to its continued success, especially in view of the technologies involved in its operations. Consequently, Federal Express continually promotes job satisfaction and advancement opportunities through personnel policies that are considered the nation's most progressive and innovative. In fact, the company is consistently included on lists of the best companies to work for in the United States.

To remain the leader in an industry that is becoming increasingly competitive, Federal Express has continued its expansion efforts. It has established domestic operations in the United Kingdom, Ireland, Belgium, Holland, and Italy, permitting overnight service within these countries. It has also expanded its operations within Canada and, through an acquisition, has extended its service coverage to the entire Caribbean. The company is also expanding into the Pacific Basin markets, with scheduled service to Tokyo. Within the United States, Federal Express is continuing to broaden its customer base and service area through expanded facilities and intensive marketing campaigns.

To support this expansion, Federal Express has invested extensive capital ($785 million during 1988) in equipment and facilities. Currently, the company has 156 aircraft on order, including four MD-11s, for delivery through 1994. The company has also added a smaller hub in Indianapolis to assist Memphis sorting operations. By the end of 1988, more than 20 percent of the company's total volume bypassed Memphis. In addition, the company is expanding its customer service centers and kiosks. Finally, Federal Express is expanding its COSMOS IIB tracking system, which instantaneously provides the shipping status of any package within its network.

The company has also pioneered new technology applications in its attempt to ensure 100 percent reliability. Advanced avionics were installed in all aircraft to permit air operations in bad weather, and most of the company's vans have been equipped with highly sophisticated computers that streamline package pickup operations. Finally, through the installation of an on-site Powership computer system, customers have been provided the capability to initiate, at their own offices, queries about package shipping status.

Federal Express has also developed a contract distribution division, which includes the PartsBank service, in which the company provides inventory management and distribution services through Federal Express facilities.

Strategic Goals

Federal Express intends to remain a leader in the express shipping industry and strives to have that leadership reflected in its earnings. To maintain leadership in the increasingly competitive express industry, Federal Express will continue to differentiate its service through market expansion and facility improvement. It will continue to broaden its U.S. service area and expand its capacity to increase U.S. market share.

The company will also continue its expansion in existing and new international markets. Together, the increased U.S. and international market bases will complement each other, creating a global express package shipment network. Federal Express views such a network as paramount for capitalizing on the trend of an increasingly global economy. The company further intends to continue developing and refining its automated tracking system and to provide additional and improved data and to support the company's international network.

The company's efforts to improve customer service responsiveness, convenience, reliability, and quality, are ongoing, and plans to identify new services, such as the PartsBank, will complement the company's overnight package service.

Federal Express projects continued and rapid growth in the industry because of the increasingly interdependent global economy and the increasing trend toward just-in-time inventory systems, in which on-hand inventories are minimal. In such cases, companies frequently rely on air express to ship smaller parts directly from the factory to the user.

Training Structure

Organization. At Federal Express, training is organized under three divisions: Air Operations, which oversees flight operations training and maintenance and engineering training; Domestic Ground Operations, which is responsible for training in domestic ground operations (mainly for couriers and customer service representatives); and Human Resource Development, which conducts all other training not specific to Air Operations and Domestic Group Operations (career development, management development, employee orientation, and consulting). Because this book is limited to technical training, this case study focuses only on Federal Express's Flight Operations training. Technical training for flight operations, maintenance and engineering, and Domestic Ground Operations is conducted independently of each area, is unique, and is targeted to specific employee groups.

The flight crew technical training group is responsible for training employees responsible for operating the company's aircraft fleet and for training employees on procedures and requirements set forth by government regulations. All training is designed, developed, produced, and presented centrally at the Memphis headquarters facility. Courseware is based on operational feedback and regulations mandated by the Federal Aviation Administration. The staff conducts all training courses, instructs in cockpit procedures, and operates Federal Express's three aircraft simulators and other cockpit training devices. The staff reports to the vice president for Flight Operations.

The maintenance and engineering technical training group trains technicians who maintain the aircraft, facilities, ground support equipment, and package-handling equipment as well as operational support personnel involved in aircraft interface (fueling, towing, and deicing). All training is designed and developed centrally at the Memphis headquarters but in a facility that is separate from the Flight Operations training facility. Training is delivered centrally at Memphis or decentrally on-site, depending upon the subject area and needs of the customer group. Ths training group reports to the vice president for engineering and heavy maintenance.

The Domestic Ground Operations technical training group is responsible for training the company's couriers, tractor trailer drivers, service agents, and ramp personnel. Although much of the training within this group involves nontechnical customer service subject matter, there is some technical training in the areas of equipment operation and package handling and computer operations (considered technical by Federal Express). Training is designed and developed centrally in Memphis by Domestic Ground Operations' instructional design systems staff and delivered centrally for Memphis-based employees and decentrally for region-based employees. The staff reports to the vice president for Domestic Ground Operations.

Staffing. The flight crew training staff is comprised of approximately 140 members, 60 of whom are support personnel. They develop, produce, and present all training curricula, operate the aircraft simulators, and develop all computer-based courses with interactive videos relating to aircraft operations. The training staff is selected on the basis of knowledge in one or more of the following areas: aircraft operations, flight computer-managed instruction, and adult learning. Instructors are selected on the basis of their background (they may be aircraft crew members, professional simulator operators, or former military pilots, flight engineers, or instructors) and indoctrinated in the company's training techniques.

The maintenance and engineering training staff is comprised of thirty-two members, of whom four are computer-enhanced training developers, eight are aircraft systems specialists, three are avionics specialists, one is an engine specialist, two are ground support equipment (GSE) specialists, two are ramp-training specialists, two are safety and health specialists, one is a facilities maintenance training specialist, and two are training specialists experienced in the new automated maintenance and material system. There are current plans to hire six more computer-enhanced training specialists. The training staff members are subject matter experts in specific areas, such as electronics, hydraulics, air-conditioning, landing gear, and fuels. The training group has been fortunate in hiring personnel with both subject matter and training experience. New trainers are indoctrinated in the maintenance and engineering group's training procedures and methodology. Aircraft maintenance and interface trainers are evenly divided between the 727 and DC-10 aircraft types.

The Domestic Ground Operations training staff is comprised of 125 members, of whom 25 are located centrally at the Memphis facility and 100 are assigned to the regional training staffs. Open training positions are made available to Federal Express employees before the company seeks outside hires. Selection is based on minimum job-specific position requirements, related communication skills, technical skills, and other management considerations such as structured panel interviews.

Target Groups. Flight Operations trains Federal Express cockpit crews as well as cockpit crews from other airlines (under contract). Subject matter concerns the operation of specific aircraft and is strictly mandated and specified by the Federal Aviation Administration.

There are five categories of flight operation training. Initial training provides new employees with operational information for specific Federal Express aircraft in which they have been previously qualified. Transition training provides flight operation training for another aircraft when a cockpit crew member changes aircraft types (for example, from a 727 to a DC-10). Upgrade training provides a flight crew member with the aircraft operating information necessary to "change seats" from a copilot to a pilot. Recurrency training is the annual proficiency training provided to all cockpit crews as per Federal Aviation Administration regulations. Recurrency training is conducted over six days, three days for classroom/computer-managed instruction and three days for aircraft simulation. Finally, difference training instructs cockpit crews in the operating procedure deviations between aircraft type models (for example, the 727-100 versus the 727-200).

Flight Operations also provides several related courses, including Inertial Navigation and Weather Radar.

Flight operation training involves the following four methods: academics, including classroom instruction and self-paced instruction that use a variety of audiovisual resources; computer-based courses with interactive video; cockpit procedure instruction; and aircraft simulation with the company's three simulators. Flight crews are actually trained by means of all four methods in a sequenced and integrated fashion. Final pilot certification in specific aircraft is accomplished via the simulators. (The pilot's first flight in a company aircraft is actually a "revenue" or cargo flight.)

The maintenance and engineering training group is responsible for training employees involved with aircraft, ground support equipment, facilities, and packaging-handling equipment and for training maintenance technicians and aircraft operational support personnel. Training topics include the following: aircraft maintenance; aircraft interface, including aircraft servicing such as fueling, deicing, and towing; facility maintenance, including air-conditioning and electrical; mechanical courses concerning equipment located at the Memphis hub and regional hubs; and the maintenance of package-handling equipment, including nonvehicle cargo equipment such as conveyor belts and rollers and movable ground support equipment.

Most training associated with aircraft maintenance and interface is required by law and is initially provided to new employees and repeated annually to ensure continued proficiency. Skill update training is also provided when new equipment is installed or procedures are implemented, as well as on-site in the field. All maintenance training for employees involved with aircraft, facilities, and package-handling equipment is provided centrally in Memphis. All aircraft interface training is conducted locally on-site by Memphis-based trainers because this training must be provided on the actual equipment in use and on the actual ramp if possible. Additionally, no single trainer on-site could be qualified to conduct training on all the interface equipment.

Package-handling equipment and facility maintenance training and safety and hazard communication training are generally provided to new employees (depending upon their experience levels) and to existing employees upon installation of new equipment. Additional training is limited to courses that address specific problems. All training courses are designed and developed on the basis of data and material provided by aircraft and equipment manufacturers.

Training within maintenance and engineering is conducted by means of three methods: classroom instruction, computer-based courses with interactive video, and on-the-job training. Specific courses may include one or more of the three methods as the needs of the group dictate.

An emerging means of training for maintenance and engineering personnel is via interactive computer terminals. Self-paced courses that rely on such terminals have maximum graphics and minimum text and allow trainees to progress according to their own proficiency levels and to repeat sections if necessary. Additionally, such training courses can be taken on-site, thereby minimizing the time away from jobs.

The maintenance and engineering training group manages its training courses with a Macintosh computer system. The computer tracks courses and attendees and monitors the use of the computer interactive video training system.

The Domestic Group Operations training group is responsible for training Federal Express's couriers, tractor trailer drivers, ramp personnel, and service agents in the areas of equipment operation, package handling, and computer operations. The larger share of technical training within this group is with couriers and service agents, who receive equipment operation, package handling, and safety instruction. Couriers and service agents also receive computer training in the operation of the automated package tracking system.

Training is generally provided upon initial employment and thereafter when new equipment is installed or new procedures are implemented. Training is conducted periodically for skill updating and recertification.

While all courses are designed and developed centrally, they are normally presented locally by the on-site training staff. All computer-based interactive video training is also designed, coordinated, and administered by the central training staff. Training methods include classroom training, on-the-job training, and computer-based interactive video instruction.

All three technical training groups use computer-assisted instruction with interactive videodisc (IVD). This system allows any trainee to take any course at his or her own pace. It also permits courses to be designed to meet the specific needs of any of the groups (for example, maintenance and engineering uses more graphics and less text). IVD also allows tailored remedial courses, where required. Finally, IVD permits training to be conducted on-site via terminals, thus minimizing the amount of time employees need to be away from their jobs. Because customer service, tight schedules, and short lead times are characteristic of the overnight package shipping business, this factor is especially critical.

Linkages. Because Federal Express's business is primarily customer service oriented, important links exist between technical and other types of training. The actual linkages depend upon the technical training group.

As part of their initial training, flight crews receive some training in the importance of customer service and their role in maintaining the tight schedules that are inherent in the overnight air package delivery business. The crews also receive an indoctrination in the company's procedures and career paths.

In addition to technical training, the Maintenance and Engineering Group also offers training in defensive driving, first aid, and cardiopulmonary resuscitation. This group also provides customer service training and an indoctrination in the company's procedures and career paths.

In the Domestic Ground Operations Group, there is an even closer link between technical training and other types of training. Close coordination among technical training, customer service training, and marketing training is crucial if Federal Express is to achieve its strategic goals of improving customer service, differentiating its service, and expanding its customer base. Since most Domestic Ground Operations employees come in contact with the customer, they must receive some customer service training.

Linkages also exist between technical training and various human resource functions. In Flight Operations, training is considered a prerequisite for promotion and increased compensation for both flight crews and aircraft maintenance personnel. In Domestic Ground Operations, a pay-for-performance system has been implemented. Employees in critical job areas must demonstrate a proficiency in certain skill areas once or twice a year (depending upon the job) in order to qualify for increased compensation.

Training Support of Strategic Goals

Technical training directly supports Federal Express's strategic goal of expansion by training flight crews to operate new aircraft and by training support personnel to operate and maintain new support equipment efficiently. In addition, technical training ensures continued proficiency in operating and maintaining existing support equipment and maintaining existing aircraft to maximize availability and reliability. The chairman of Federal Express is very committed to the use of technical training to help the company achieve its strategic goals. In fact, he is the catalyst behind the computer-based, interactive video training program that is being installed throughout the company.

Ford Motor Company

Ford Motor Company is the second-largest U.S. corporation and one of the "big three" of U.S. automobile manufacturers. Through its global manufacturing and marketing operations, it serves more than 200 countries and territories. In addition to being a major producer of cars, trucks, and farm equipment, Ford is involved in aerospace technologies, defense-related research, communications, land development, and financial services. During 1988, the company continued its record performance by attaining a net income of $5.3 billion (an increase of 15 percent from a year earlier) on sales of $92.4 billion (an increase of 16 percent). Ford employs 350,000 people throughout its worldwide operations.

As a result of a recent restructuring, Ford's eleven divisions and sixty-three subsidiaries are organized within three major business operation areas. The Automotive Operations Area contains all U.S. and international automobile and truck operations. The Diversified Products Operations Area encompasses two main groups of businesses. First, it includes the Automotive

Components Product Group, which produces a variety of automotive material ranging from iron castings and plastics to electronic engine controls and radiators. Second, it includes several nonautomotive businesses, such as Ford Aerospace Corporation, Ford Motor Land Development, Ford New Holland (the third-largest manufacturer of farm equipment in the free world), Ford Glass Division (the second-largest glass manufacturer in the United States), and the Rouge Steel Company (the eighth-largest steel producer in the United States). The Financial Services Group is Ford's third major business operations area and consists of the company's First Nationwide Financial Corporation as well as Ford's credit, insurance, and leasing operations.

As part of the U.S. automobile industry, Ford experienced the same decline that characterized the industry during the 1970s and early 1980s. During that period, oil prices continued to escalate, and by the late 1970s, the industry slipped into a recession along with the rest of the economy. Consumer tastes were also changing as reflected in the increased demand for vehicles with better quality, style, fuel efficiency, and handling performance. The "big three" automobile manufacturers, however, were relatively inattentive to the changing tastes and consumer demands. As a result, Japanese automobile manufacturers, who were producing more stylish and fuel-efficient automobiles with good quality and performance, gained a significant market share during the period. Prior to the industry recovery during the mid-1980s, the entire U.S. automobile industry lost billions of dollars. Ford, alone, lost almost $4 billion between 1980 and 1982.

Ford's recovery and performance during the past several years has been outstanding. Its automotive market share has increased dramatically, reflecting an ability to design and develop products that target its customers' demand for quality, performance, and style. During 1987, Ford continued to increase its U.S. automotive market share, with increases of 2 percent (to a total of 20.2 percent) for cars and 1 percent (to a total of 29.1 percent) for trucks. These increases represent a significant achievement considering the intensely competitive nature of the industry. To maintain its strong competitive position, Ford has continued to invest heavily in new automotive designs and technologies as well as in new plant and equipment technologies. In 1987 alone, the company allocated $3.6 billion for capital investments.

Ford's dramatic recovery can also be attributed to a rigorous cost reduction program that has decreased annual costs by more than $5 billion since 1980. Between 1978 and 1985, this program reduced overall employment by 28 percent and eliminated several management layers. Further reductions are planned through 1990. These reductions together with new technology equipment and procedures have enabled Ford to increase its productivity and achieve a profit level greater than its rival, General Motors, with a lower unit sales volume.

A key factor in Ford's recovery and subsequent success has been a new corporate culture that was created during the early 1980s by its then corporate president, Donald Petersen. Contrasting significantly with the previous corporate climate of bureaucratic management, limited creativity, alienated workers, and customer unresponsiveness, the new culture promotes teamwork, cooperation, participation, and trust among employees, unions, suppliers, and dealers. The underlying philosophy of the new environment is that no one individual is responsible for designing, engineering, manufacturing, assembling, and selling a product. Only through teamwork and the full participation of all employees in all product phases can Ford succeed in the future. Its Taurus and Sable automobiles represent the tremendous success of such a team effort in creating a totally new car design that incorporates the styling, performance, and quality demanded by the customer.

Ford continues to promote the new culture through its Participative Management and Employee Involvement programs. Nearly all Ford managers and supervisors have received training in participative management to learn how to involve employees in setting goals, making decisions, solving problems, and planning. The company also stresses employee involvement, which encourages employees to assume a greater role in the decision-making process. This new participative environment at Ford is supported by many of the company's educational and training programs, which are designed to broaden employee skills, expand job capabilities, and enhance personal growth and development.

The company's unions have also increased their level of participation within the new corporate culture. In fact, the UAW-Ford "Best-in-Class" Quality Program, which created a joint permanent team to develop quality-related training for employees, is the product of a 1987 labor agreement.

The new environment at Ford has been a major factor in the company's recovery and continues to contribute to its success. It is actively supported by its founder, Chairman Donald Petersen (who became CEO in 1985), all levels of management, and even the labor unions.

Strategic Goals

Ford's overall corporate objective is to improve quality, increase productivity, reduce costs, develop new competitive products, and involve people at all levels. Each of the three business operation areas has established specific strategic goals pertaining to its product group.

The Automotive Operations Area has established the goal of becoming a low-cost producer of high-quality and appealing products that respond to customers' needs and desires in every market in which Ford does business. To improve product quality and competitiveness, the Automotive Operations Area has initiated the ALPHA Project, considered to be one of Ford's most important and advanced projects. Under this project, all elements of the automotive product and manufacturing techniques are examined to identify better ways to build vehicles that are leaders in cost and quality. To date, the ALPHA Project can be attributed to the following concepts: modular construction, automated body welding, flexible machinery, automated guided vehicles, vision robots, and just-in-time inventories. The ALPHA Project will continue to play a major role in helping the Automotive Operations Area achieve its goals.

The Automotive Operations Area also intends to continue its "centers of excellence" concept, which provides for the sharing of Ford's worldwide automotive design and production resources. Under this concept, Automotive Operations is able to employ the best resources worldwide and, at the same time, reduce costs and eliminate duplication. Ford has developed the Worldwide Engineering Releasing System to facilitate resource sharing by providing an automated link between North American and overseas manufacturing and engineering groups. To remain viable in the increasingly competitive and global economy, Ford plans to increase the use of resource sharing in the future.

Consistent with the new corporate culture, the Automotive Operations Area will continue to conceptualize, design, develop, manufacture, and market vehicles through an aided manufacturing (CAD/CAM) and thus will assume a greater role in the integrated design-to-engineering-to-manufacturing process.

Automotive Operations also plans to pursue more cooperative agreements with other automotive manufacturers, such as Mazda, to capitalize on the technical and manufacturing synergies of the two companies. The jointly owned Ford/Mazda plant, which produces both Ford and Mazda vehicles, is an example of such an agreement.

The Diversified Products Operations Area is pursuing the strategic goal of competing successfully worldwide within each group of businesses by providing high-quality, cost-competitive products that meet customers' needs. To help accomplish this goal, several units within this operation area will be expanded and several other units will be modernized.

Overall, the primary objective of the Financial Services Group is to provide a source of stable earnings to counter the cyclical nature of Ford's automotive business. Its main strategy is to broaden the markets of its banking, insurance, credit, and leasing businesses by adding new, related businesses. It also strives to provide the best value to its customers through efficient operation and service.

Within all three of its business operation areas, Ford intends to continue expanding and improving its Participative Management and Employee Involvement Programs. The company believes that only with a well-trained and broadly skilled and motivated work force that functions with management as a team can the company succeed in the highly competitive and increasingly global economy.

Training Structure

Organization. The education and training functions within Ford are largely decentralized according to the specific requirements of its individual worldwide components. Certain aspects of the company's development efforts — such as those for the top 2,000 senior executives — have very concentrated programs that are offered by dedicated organizations such as the Executive Development Center located in Detroit, Michigan. This center provides a carefully selected range of offerings for Ford's top management and serves as a focal point for the acquisition of a "total perspective" on the business. In addition, unique niche programs examine aspects of the business in which, for example, leadership, strategic decision making, or association strategy may be a key factor in the long-term success of the enterprise. The design of executive development programs emphasizes teamwork and participation as important features of the learning experience.

Although much of the training at Ford is accomplished decentrally at the division and plant levels, several broad-based training functions have been assigned to the Management and Technical Training Department, located centrally at the Human Resources Development Center in Dearborn, Michigan. The training department, which is organized under the Personnel and Organization office of the Ford North American Automotive Operations, provides training in three major areas: management (below the senior level), technical, and apprentice and launch. In terms of central training, this discussion is limited to a review of the technical and apprentice and launch training sections because management training is generally less technical in nature.

The training provided by the central technical training section is concentrated in generic courses that are relevant to several of the company's divisions. The intent is to minimize the duplication of training effort related to subject matter that applies to many divisions (such as Allen Bradley programmable logic controllers, which are used in many of the company's plants). All phases of training, from needs analysis, design, development, and validation through delivery and evaluation, are accomplished centrally.

The central apprentice and launch training section is responsible for administering and coordinating the Apprentice and Launch programs. For the Apprentice Program, the central staff works closely with the Ford-UAW Joint Apprenticeship Committee, which determines national program standards and content, coordinates the on-the-job training segment with the individual plants at which it is provided, and screens area community colleges for potential sources of the formal classroom instruction segment of the program. For the Launch Program, which provides training in support of plant expansion and the launching of new products, the staff coordinates and oversees the efforts of a training team that is temporarily assigned to a plant to conduct initial training and to establish a supporting training program and organization.

The bulk of the training at Ford, however, is decentralized to the individual plants because most are involved in specialized products, functions, and missions. The plants are considered to be the most knowledgeable in terms of their own unique operations and consequently the best equipped to develop and conduct training programs. Although there is some variation among the company's fifty-three manufacturing and assembly plants, each plant generally has a small training staff that is organized under the plant's Employee Relations Department. Each plant training staff is responsible for accomplishing all phases of training for subject matter that is specific to its particular plant.

To provide a specific example of plant training, we will review the training operations of the Ford Climate Control Division's Sheldon Road plant. The division consists of two U.S. and several overseas plants. The primary responsibility of the training staff at the Sheldon Road plant is to support the plant's training needs. The staff may, however, provide assistance, upon request, to the division's other U.S. plant training staff.

Staffing. The Management and Technical Training Department's Technical Training Section has ten full-time staff members with specialties in instructional system design, engineering, skilled trades, management development, training program administration, consulting, and computer learning. The Technical Training Section uses outside sources, such as consultants and area educational institutions, almost exclusively to meet its training needs. Training staff members serve as "minimanagers" over the contracted efforts to design, develop, deliver, and evaluate training courseware. Most staff members are responsible for managing several of the many training programs that are being designed and developed by approximately twenty-five outside consultants. Extensive use of external resources increases the company's flexibility tremendously and enables more training programs to be developed.

The technical training staff does, however, accomplish most of the needs analysis in-house through the periodic review of select companywide operations and continuous interaction with line personnel. Staff expertise in engineering and the skilled trades facilitates the review process and enhances the credibility of the training function when dealing with line operations.

Presentation of the training programs is provided through three sources. The technical training staff may elect to deliver select training courseware in-house at the Human Resources Development Center. Training consultants may be contracted to conduct training, either at the Human Resources Development Center or at some off-site facility. Finally, through long-term agreements with several area universities and colleges, such as Eastern Michigan University in Ypsilanti, Michigan, and the Lawrence Technological University in Southfield, Michigan, instructional support may be provided by educational institutions.

The Apprentice and Launch Section of the Management and Technical Training Department has a full-time staff of eighteen employees. The Ford-UAW Joint Apprenticeship Committee, represented by five management members and five union members, administers the Apprentice Program's overall standards and provides direction and guidance based on those standards. The committee meets formally each month and inforally as needed to address issues concerning the Apprentice Program's structure and content. The committee administers and coordinates the program throughout the parent company to ensure that apprentices receive the appropriate formal classroom instruction at area community colleges and follow the proper job progression during their apprenticeship training.

The staff coordinates the program with individual plant joint apprenticeship subcommittees, which oversee both the on-the-job training segment at their plants and the formal classroom instruction segment at area community colleges. (Each plant has a joint apprenticeship subcommittee consisting of one management and one union employee.) The subcommittee is further responsible for recommending to the national committee the best community colleges to serve as providers for the formal classroom instruction segment and for continually monitoring the instruction to ensure that it meets program objectives.

The central apprenticeship training staff is also responsible for the design and development of most of the courseware that is used at the plants to complement the on-the-job training segment. The staff may develop the courseware in-house with its own resources or externally through outside consultants.

The apprentice and launch section training staff also provides a resource for administering launch training programs by overseeing and coordinating a launch team's development of a training function within plants. The launch team is responsible for creating a training plan, developing initial training programs, and establishing a permanent training organization in each plant to which it is assigned. After the new product is successfully introduced, the launch team transfers training responsibilties to the plant's training organization and departs the plant.

The Technical Training Group at the Sheldon Road plant consists of four full-time staff members who have subject matter and human resource development expertise. The plant training staff is supplemented by several line employees who have training experience and have taken the initiative to design, develop, and deliver several training courses. The training staff is responsible for all phases of training for courseware that is either plant-specific or generic but plant-related. With its own resources, the staff accomplishes most of the training needs analysis but only a limited amount of training design, development, and delivery. (It is generally limited to videotape training to address new equipment setup, operation, and maintenance or operational problems and classroom instruction for special courses.) The majority of the training is accomplished through outside sources, such as original equipment manufacturers, consultants, and educational institutions, under the management and direction of the training staff. The degree of outsourcing depends on the specific course. Some courses are outsourced in their entirety; in other courses, specific phases or parts of phases are outsourced. Training delivery may be provided at the plant by the staff or a contractor or at an off-site facility by an outside provider.

A joint training committee at the Sheldon Road plant serves as an advisory panel over the plant's technical training group. The committee, which is comprised of twelve members from production, engineering, and training (a plant training specialist cochairs the committee with an hourly employee), provides guidance and direction to the plant training operations. Each committee member is supported by a subcommittee consisting of personnel from the member's area of responsibility. The subcommittees continually search their respective areas for potential problems or opportunities that could be addressed through training. The training committee meets twice a month to review and discuss training issues (such as operational problems or planned new equipment and procedures) that have been identified by the various members and their subcommittees and to determine appropriate training solutions. These solutions are expanded into a general training plan, which serves as a guide for the plant training staff when it designs and develops specific courseware. The committee provides a mechanism for the plant line personnel, including engineers and skilled employees, to become more actively involved with training personnel in the training development process.

The plant technical training staff has the additional responsibility of overseeing the Apprenticeship Program's on-the-job training segment, which is conducted at the plant, and the formal instruction segment, which is provided by area community colleges. The staff coordinates the on-the-job training on the plant floor to ensure that apprentices make the proper rotation among the plant's different departments and equipment. The staff also conducts select on-site training, such as classroom or video instruction, that may be required by the central apprenticeship training staff during the on-the-job training segment. Additionally, the plant training staff monitors the formal instruction segment to ensure that apprentices attend and satisfactorily complete the appropriate courses. The Apprenticeship Program at the plant is guided by the plant joint apprenticeship subcommittee.

Target Groups. Within the Management and Technical Training Department, the Technical Training Section provides training to Ford's approximately 8,000 manufacturing, engineering, and other technical professionals (some courses are attended by product engineers) and its approximately 19,000 skilled (journeyman-level) trade workers. Of the eighty-eight generic courses offered by technical training, approximately fifty-four are for manufacturing, engineering, and other technical professionals, and thirty-four are for skilled trade workers. The courses for manufacturing, engineering, and other technical professionals involve all functions associated with manufacturing as well as the various aspects of industrial, plant, process, and maintenance engineering. The courses for skilled trade workers cover troubleshooting, microcomputers, robot maintenance, and variable-speed motors. Courses are designed and developed as a result of a needs analysis conducted by the training staff or in response to requests received from division or plant training coordinators. Following discussions with the training coordinators and, in some cases, plant visits, training staff members determine whether the proposed training addresses a problem or need of several divisions or plants; if so, it is developed.

The technical training staff employs classroom instruction, computer-based training (there are seventy such training systems), and interactive videodisc systems (there are fifteen videodisc systems) in its various courseware. Classroom instruction is used primarily for subject matter that experiences rapid changes (and therefore does not justify the high development costs for computer-based or interactive training programs) or that is relatively basic in nature. Classroom instruction is used frequently for engineers. The self-paced computer-based instruction with interactive video tends to be most commonly used for training skilled trade workers, although it is also used to train engineering and technical professionals in computer applications. Although much of the training is conducted on-site at the Human Resources Development Center, some training is delivered off-site through the purchase of computer-based and interactive videodisc materials from the Human Resources Development Center, training consultants, or educational institutions.

At the Sheldon Road plant, technical training primarily involves the technical professional and skilled tradesman. Generally, training is developed in response to an issue or opportunity uncovered by the plant's joint training committee or the plant training staff. The subject matter frequently involves new equipment, new hire and job rotation, or remedial and job skill update training. With new equipment, the plant trainers work closely with the original equipment manufacturers to develop training for the equipment prior to its installation date. The original equipment manufacturer may be required to provide training either at the manufacturer's plant or the Sheldon Road plant, or the plant training staff may decide to conduct the training on-site. In some cases, the training staff may visit the original equipment manufacturer's plant to develop a video course on the operation and maintenance of the new equipment. The plant training staff is also in the process of enhancing the new hire and job rotation training. By the end of 1989, the staff will have completed an effort to establish training requirements and objectives for all of the plant's job classifications. Finally, the training staff is involved with remedial or skill update training in response to specific production or equipment operation problems. Several members of the training committee and subcommittees and several line employees have assisted the training staff by developing training programs to address specific operating problems in their respective areas of responsibility.

To deliver the training, the plant training staff employs classroom and videotape instruction and interactive videodisc. Videotape is the preferred medium and the one most widely used at the plant. The use of interactive videodisc is relatively new and is currently limited to seven or eight generic training programs encompassing electronics, hydraulics, and microprocessors. Training may be accomplished in-house or by an outside provider at the plant or at an off-site facility.

Linkages. There is only an indirect link between technical and other types of training at Ford. Management and supervisory training, although not entirely technical, does emphasize the need for greater teamwork and involvement by all employees. To maximize this involvement, each employee must be fully trained in a broadly based task area. Additionally, with decision making now being required at lower levels in the organization, employees must have the requisite decision-making skills. Management and supervisory training reinforces this new participatory culture and emphasizes the fact that line managers are also responsible for ensuring that their employees are properly trained.

Ford's Apprenticeship Program creates a direct link between technical training and the human resource function. The program's structure and content are negotiated and agreed upon by mangement and union representatives. In addition, progress through and completion of apprenticeship training directly affects promotion, compensation, and other human resource functions.

Training Support of Strategic Goals

Ford believes that to achieve its strategic goals in each of its three operation areas, it must have a dedicated, skilled, and motivated work force. The company believes that through participatory management and employee involvement, it can develop such a work force and maximize the benefits available from its skills, knowledge, and capabilities. Technical training directly supports the company's new culture by providing the range and depth of skills required for workplace participation.

Ford is committed to both employee involvement and training as means of maintaining its successful performance.

The Technical Training Sections are the company leaders in the area of evaluation. All courses are evaluated at Level I (reaction questionnaire) and Level II (before and after questions). Ten to fifteen courses are evaluated each year by an outside training vendor at Level III (application to the job) and Level IV for bottom-line results. Courses are not put on-line until they have satisfied the validation criteria of 90/90, that is, until 90 percent of the participants achieve 90 percent of the course objectives.

Because of Ford's emphasis on process and continuous improvements, the section has linked up with the Instructional Technology Department at Wayne State University. Candidates in the master's and doctoral programs are employed part-time to conduct course integrity evaluations on technical courses.

CHAPTER 6

Best Practices
in Technical Training:
Integrated Systems

This chapter profiles five companies with training delivery systems that have both centralized and decentralized features. Each of these companies has a strong central training function, but each one's various divisions also play a large role in training. In all five companies, training is conducted at both the corporate and division levels. The companies discussed in this chapter are FMC Corporation, Frito-Lay, Inc., Merck Pharmaceutical Manufacturing Division, Motorola, and Northern Telecom.

FMC Corporation

FMC Corporation is one of the world's leading producers of machinery and chemicals for industry, government, and agriculture. The company participates on a worldwide basis in selected segments of five broad markets: industrial chemicals, precious metals, defense systems, performance chemicals, and machinery and equipment.

In 1988, FMC reported sales of $3.3 billion, an increase of 5 percent from 1987. Reported net income declined between 1987 and 1988. However, excluding the gain from the public issuance of 7.5 million shares of FMC Gold Company stock in 1987, net income actually rose to $129 million in 1988 from $96 million in 1987 — a 34 percent jump. This dramatic increase was the result of higher earnings from FMC's chemical and precious metal businesses combined with lower interest expense.

In 1988, FMC also achieved an annual return on investment of more than 15 percent for the fifth straight year. The company's continued success reflects a concerted effort to improve the performance of its businesses, to reduce working capital, and to redirect capital toward high-return uses.

The company likewise focused on careful deployment of FMC's financial assets. Its pension plan restructuring, for example, returned more than $340 million and 11.3 million shares of FMC stock to the corporation. FMC has also pursued innovative financial strategies, including the public offering of FMC Gold Company stock, the first major Dutch auction self-tender, and the 1986 recapitalization.

The repatriation of excess cash from foreign subsidiaries and cash generated from operations allowed FMC to reduce debt and trade receivables financing by more than $170 million in 1988. Since the company's May 1986 recapitalization, FMC has reduced debt and other obligations by more than $750 million, or nearly 40 percent of the debt associated with the recapitalization. At the end of 1988, total debt stood at $1.5 billion. Principal payments will continue to reduce this debt, although no significant payments are required until mid-1992.

At the same time, capital expenditures increased 19 percent to $186 million in 1988. Expansion of the company's chemical and precious metal operations and the installation of new manufacturing systems in its defense and machinery businesses accounted for the increased spending. In 1989 capital outlays were projected to rise again, to $275 million, as FMC continued to pursue new investment opportunities.

Research and development expenditures for 1988 rose 9 percent to $144 million and were focused on developing and testing new agricultural chemicals and improving FMC's defense system capabilities. FMC spends nearly twice as much as the average industrial company on research and development and believes that such investment will generate new and innovative products for the company. Funding was expected to rise slightly in 1989.

FMC employs approximately 24,000 people in its eighty-eight manufacturing facilities and mines, which are located in twenty-four states and fourteen foreign countries.

The company's industrial chemicals businesses manufacture a wide variety of chemicals, including soda ash, phosphates, hydrogen peroxide, and lithium. Major customers include detergent, glass, and paper producers as well as food processors and other chemical companies.

FMC's precious metal business is dominated by its 89 percent stake in FMC Gold Company, which mines gold and silver and ranks first among major North American gold companies in return on investment and among the leaders in net income.

FMC's defense system business develops, manufactures, and supplies ground combat vehicles and naval weapons systems to the armed forces of the United States and other free world governments.

FMC's performance chemicals business develops, manufactures, and markets proprietary specialty chemicals for the agricultural, food, and pharmaceutical industries.

Machinery and equipment businesses provide specialized machinery to the food, petroleum, and material-handling industries and to municipalities. Most of these businesses command strong positions in specialized markets.

Strategic Goals

Driving the strategy of each business is one overriding goal: "becoming our customers' most valued supplier." In the years since FMC adopted this goal, the corporation has seen its employees steadily gain a deeper insight into the needs of its customers, the strategies of its businesses, and the demands of a highly competitive global market.

FMC's major challenge for the future will be to continue operating its businesses efficiently — maintaining high returns and paying off debt — while at the same time generating sufficient new opportunities to bring investments more in line with FMC's cash-generating capabilities.

To address that challenge, FMC is stepping up efforts to

identify opportunities that meet its high-return requirements and offer a sustainable competitive advantage in businesses it understands. The company is building on its strengths: strong market shares, low-cost positions, strong relationships with key customers, technical and financial expertise, worldwide presence, capable and experienced management, and dedicated employees.

Training Structure

Organization. Technical training at FMC is organized on two levels: corporate and field. At the corporate level, four areas of focus exist within their own functions: manufacturing, information resources, finance, and engineering. All are staffed by field-experienced employees with successful records of line achievement. They work with FMC organizations around the world. At the field level, FMC groups and divisions tap the corporate-based functional training as well as design their own technical programs in response to needs assessments.

Functional-based technical training is supported by the Corporate Training and Development Department, which is located at FMC world headquarters in Chicago, Illinois. This department is one of the human resource functions. Corporate Training and Development focuses primarily on nontechnical training and a full range of employee and organization development activities. The department also acts as an internal consultant to the technical training developers at both the field and corporate levels.

Manufacturing technical training provided from corporate is designed or selected by a team of managers who rotate into the corporate role to provide leadership and innovation. The team addresses such topics as quality, safety, manufacturing resource planning, and statistical process control. The department also maintains a video and computer-based learning library, stocked by contracted vendors who provide both customized and off-the-shelf packages.

Information systems technical training provides software training by means of programs that are in general use throughout the company. The staff's expertise in systems design and software applications enables them to consult corporationwide on both software and hardware issues.

Engineering and finance focus on continuing education more than on skill-based technical training, although both are addressed in their activities. The Corporate Finance Department provides training for both financial and nonfinancial managers. The Central Engineering Laboratory, a corporate function based in Santa Clara, California, ensures state-of-the-art engineering capabilities through its consulting and technical training efforts. Engineers and staff specialists serve as trainers in more than thirty courses and custom design courses as well.

The Corporate Training and Development Department takes both a reactive and proactive stance. It is reactive in the sense that it responds to requests from divisions for assistance with needs assessments; special training requirements, such as foreign language training; and identification of resources that can be used when establishing new divisional training. The department also acts as a training clearinghouse for the entire corporation. It maintains libraries of generic training resources and makes them available to all divisions. In addition, it tracks all training completed at the divisional level and provides data to other divisions with similar training needs.

The Corporate Training Development Department's proactive stance permits its team to design and develop training, career development programs, and on-the-job training programs on macro issues that extend beyond specific division or group operations. Courses may be developed in technical or nontechnical areas on the basis of the department's own initiative or in response to a requirement from the corporation's divisions or groups.

In its capacity as consultant to all divisions and groups within the corporation, the Corporate Training and Development Department lends considerable expertise in all areas of training. This expertise is particularly important because most divisions do not have fully staffed training functions.

Of all of FMC's groups, only Defense Systems and Petroleum Equipment have well-defined, fully staffed training and development functions. Both groups do most of their own skill-based training as well as long-range planning for training development and implementation.

Within these two groups, technical training is important as a coordinator and overseer of employee training. For example, within the Petroleum Equipment group, training is centralized for design and development and for train-the-trainer instruction. Delivery, however, is decentralized to the regions (Singapore, London, and Houston).

Staffing. Like many corporations, FMC utilizes a relatively small number of trainers both at headquarters and its divisions. (The Corporate Training and Development Department is staffed with four full-time employees.) The corporation relies on some outside contractors but predominantly on operations personnel to provide much of the training expertise. Staff members at headquarters and lower organizational levels coordinate courses that are designed and developed by vendors. They also serve as design specialists for courses developed in-house. While many of FMC's divisions rely on headquarters to provide much of their training, those divisions with fully staffed training functions design and develop in-house courses through the joint efforts of a trainer and a subject matter expert.

Technical training is predominately delivered in the field. Courses that are designed and developed centrally are delivered locally upon request. At the division level, courses are frequently delivered by line mangers because they are most credible to the learners and have experience with the corporation's products and operations.

In addition to in-house training, FMC encourages all of its employees to seek outside professional development by providing 85 percent reimbursement for all coursework and 100 percent reimbursement for degree programs.

Target Groups. FMC is diverse in nature. Training is a team effort shared by manager and employee. Training for target groups varies according to the nature of the operation as well as individual needs. For example, the Defense Systems Group concentrates on technical training and professional development opportunities for technicians and technical professionals. This enables technical employees to be up-to-date on new operations and procedures, and it fulfills the group's contractual requirements for training. Technical training within the Petroleum Equipment Group, however, is reserved for setup, operations, and maintenance personnel, who must keep abreast of specific processes and procedures as they relate to operations. Technical professionals in this group receive more training in nontechnical areas, such as interpersonal skills and management development.

Exceptions to shifting the training emphasis according to operational requirements can be found in several key areas. Safety, hazard communication, and other kinds of training mandated by regulation or contract are conducted with all affected personnel as required. Additionally, headquarters occasionally requires some special types of training for all company personnel.

Linkages. FMC previously separated its various types of training. Increased emphasis on customer service coupled with product knowledge has resulted in stronger links between marketing, customer service, interpersonal skills, and management development. These linkages are important for technical professionals as well as customer-interface employees. There is a strong link between training and the company's performance management process, which identifies specific employee weaknesses that training can address.

Training Support of Strategic Goals

Technical training at FMC directly supports the corporation's strategies by providing its employees with the skills to lead the competition in the international marketplace. As FMC continues its streamlining effort by restructuring and introducing new technologies to increase productivity, technical training is increasingly critical to work force development.

Technical training also plays an important role in supporting FMC's goal of identifying and developing new business opportunities. New and incumbent workers must be trained in the venture's operations and procedures.

The third way in which technical training supports FMC's strategic goals is by providing operational skills and product knowledge to all employees. These skills and knowledge are of particular importance when employees are dealing with customers, identifying potential new markets, and responding to challenges posed by FMC's competitors.

Frito-Lay/PepsiCo Inc.

Frito-Lay, Inc., is a wholly owned subsidiary of PepsiCo, Inc., which is a large food and beverage company operating in the soft drink, restaurant, and snack food business areas. PepsiCo operates more than 1,000 bottling plants, which process products for the domestic and international markets. PepsiCo brands represent one-third of the U.S. soft drink market. In its restaurant business area, PepsiCo operates the largest restaurant system in the world, which consists of the Kentucky Fried Chicken, Pizza Hut, and Taco Bell chains. Within PepsiCo's snack food business area, Frito-Lay is the nation's largest manufacturer and marketer of salty snacks. During 1987, PepsiCo earned $594.8 million in net income (an increase of 30 percent over 1986) on sales of $11.5 billion (an increase of 26 percent). PepsiCo employs approximately 225,000 people worldwide.

Overall, PepsiCo's three business areas achieved record sales and operating profits during 1987. In each area, PepsiCo's businesses successfully increased sales volumes and gained market share by capitalizing on excellent brand recognition and the company's comprehensive domestic and international sales and distribution network. Moreover, each of PepsiCo's businesses continued to reduce costs and increase operating efficiencies in a major companywide effort to improve profit margins.

PepsiCo's margins were also enhanced by the 1986 acquisition of Kentucky Fried Chicken, MEI Corporation, and Seven-Up International. Because these three companies were acquired for their financial strengths and potential synergies, they were quickly assimilated into PepsiCo's operations. As a result, the companies began contributing immediately to PepsiCo's total earnings.

Expansion in sales volume and market share can also be attributed to the nature of PepsiCo's products and to the habits of its consumers. Although popular with all ages, the company's products tend to be most heavily consumed by teenagers and young adults. The increased consumption of snack foods and soft drinks began with the baby-boom generation and, to the benefit of the company, has continued as that generation has aged. PepsiCo also has targeted the baby-boomers' changing life-style with a network of restaurants that offer fast foods and carry-out service. These consumption habits are continuing with a new generation of soft drink, snack food, and fast-food consumers.

PepsiCo has also been successful in targeting specific consumers with existing products and product variations. For example, the company promotes Diet Pepsi to its older weight-conscious customers and regular Pepsi to its younger customers. It also has responded to regional tastes by introducing variations of existing products, such as Cajun spice flavored Ruffles potato chips. Because of the vitality of its products, PepsiCo has been able to develop line extensions of existing products, which require less investment and involve lower risks.

Frito-Lay and PepsiCo Foods International make up PepsiCo's snack food business area. Frito-Lay employs approximately 26,000 people (10,000 of whom are involved in sales), has numerous manufacturing facilities around the country, and over 1,000 distribution centers. During 1987, Frito-Lay achieved total sales of $3.7 billion, which was an increase of 6 percent over the previous year and the nineteenth consecutive year of increased sales. Its major brands experienced significant increases in sales volume during 1987, and four of its brands, Doritos tortilla chips, Lay's and Ruffles potato chips, and Fritos corn chips were in the top ten sales volume for all dry food brands sold in U.S. food stores.

As with PepsiCo, a great deal of Frito-Lay's success is attributable to a general changing of life-style and consumption habits in the United States. Today's consumers actually eat more salty snacks than did consumers of the same age a decade ago. In fact, today's forty-year-old consumes approximately four pounds more salty food snacks annually than did his or her counterpart a decade ago. This trend began with the baby-boom generation and has continued as that generation has aged. New generations, especially today's teenagers, who are the largest consumers of snack foods, actually eat more snack foods than did any previous generation of teens. Overall, the U.S. per capita consumption of salty snack foods is twelve pounds per year.

Frito-Lay's comprehensive and highly efficient manufacturing, sales, and distribution networks have also contributed to its strong performance. During 1987, it actually reduced operating expenses by $150 million through increased efficiency and productivity. New equipment, such as the hand-held computer that the Frito-Lay sales force uses to track orders, monitor product sales, and evaluate sales promotions, was developed to reduce paperwork and associated costs. This is a critical factor with Frito-Lay's 10,000-person sales force, which services 400,000 accounts. Frito-Lay's sales force also stocks the snack foods directly on supermarket shelves (where most salty snack foods are sold), enabling the company to maintain very close inventory control and to ensure product freshness. It also reduces supermarkets' labor costs, which together with high sales volumes makes Frito-Lay snacks some of the most profitable dry food brands sold in supermarkets.

As a result of its efficient distribution network, aggressive marketing programs, and extremely popular food products, Frito-Lay has achieved annual product sales volume increases during each of the last five years.

Strategic Goals

PepsiCo's overall strategy is to retain its leadership position in soft drinks, snack foods, and restaurants. It intends to concentrate its managerial and financial resources on expanding product lines within these three rapidly growing business areas. The company also intends to pursue growth through carefully selected acquisitions related to its three business areas.

To maintain its leadership in the snack food business area, Frito-Lay will capitalize on Americans' increased consumption of snack foods. It will increase market share by segmenting its

markets and then targeting specific products or product variations toward each market segment. Its primary emphasis will be
to provide quality snacks in flavors that all consumers will enjoy.

Frito-Lay will also concentrate on improving productivity
and decreasing costs through a continuing review of its total
operations to identify areas that can be made more efficient.
Additionally, through the Methods Improvement Program, the
company will encourage its employees to suggest procedures and
techniques that will increase productivity or improve product
quality.

Training Structure

Organization. At Frito-Lay, technical training is conducted by two major groups: a central training staff, which is
located at Frito-Lay's headquarters, and individual training
staffs, which are located on-site at the company's various plants
and distribution facilities. The central training staff is generally
responsible for designing and developing training courses for
the individual sites and for overall administration of the technical
training function. Each of Frito-Lay's forty plants has on-site
training staffs that conduct the actual training and evaluate the
training courses. The company's distribution facilities also conduct some training; however, the major emphasis is with the
plants. The central training staff reports through the Human
Resources Department, whereas the individual on-site training
staffs report through their respective plant managers. Although
there is no direct reporting structure between the central and
on-site trainers, they do work closely during the needs analysis
and design and development phases. The on-site trainers also
provide continual feedback to the central staff concerning the
effectiveness of the training in meeting its objectives. In addition to its design and development responsibilities, the central
staff is available to assist individual sites in identifying and resolv-
ing training problems.

Frito-Lay's training structure (centrally designed, developed, and administered but decentrally delivered) is not considered typical of the food-processing industry, in which most

companies are small. Training in the smaller companies is usually informal, consisting of casual on-the-job training. Frito-Lay's
training structure, however, best satisfies its needs and provides
three major benefits. First, central control, design, and development ensures that training will support the corporate strategic
goals. With decentralized control and development, training programs tend to be less focused on the company's central objectives and policies. Second, centralized design and development
increases training efficiency by reducing staff duplication, while
at the same time, decentralized delivery allows the various individual sites to customize courses to meet specific needs. Decentralized delivery is consistent with Frito-Lay's Self-Reliance
Program, which encourages increased autonomy at the company's plants. Third, decentralized delivery of training at the
plant level enables the target groups to receive a greater share
of hands-on training and to reduce the amount of time required
away from the job for training.

Staffing. The central training staff consists of seventeen
members, each selected for his or her background in adult education and experience in training design and development. Staff
members include professional engineers and managers with
direct experience in food processing and manufacturing. Approximately 50 percent of the present central trainers obtained
training from other Frito-Lay operations, while the other trainers
were hired from outside the company. Each of the trainers has
been employed at Frito-Lay for more than six years.

Each of the individual plants and distribution facilities
has a training staff that ranges from one to four members. Depending on the function of the individual facility, the staffs conduct training programs in the areas of manufacturing, processing,
maintenance, distribution, and marketing. The greatest number
of on-site trainers (approximately 175) conduct manufacturing,
processing, and maintenance training because Frito-Lay's greatest emphasis is in these areas. Site trainers are professionals
and supervisors who are selected for their knowledge of the processes and operations in which training is required. The staff
selection process begins at the plant level, where individuals are

nominated on the basis of performance and knowledge. Each candidate's name and background data are then submitted to central training, which reviews the candidate's background to determine suitability. Upon selection, the candidate is enrolled in central training's Instructors' Certification Workshop (train-the-trainer program). The candidate is next required to make a presentation before a jury and then, if approved, becomes certified and is transferred to his or her plant's training department.

Target Groups. At Frito-Lay, technical professionals, technicians, and craft workers receive technical training. The technical professionals located at individual plants and facilities receive the least amount of training because they are primarily engineers and managers with background knowledge and experience. Their training consists of an initial operation overview followed by periodic new equipment or procedure familiarization. Technical professionals located at Frito-Lay's headquarters also receive some technical training. Because they are primarily researchers and scientists engaged in complex technologies, however, their technical training consists of professional development in their respective fields and is normally provided by major universities. Training for headquarters-based technical professionals is administered by the research department separately from other technical training.

Most of Frito-Lay's technical training involves technicians and craft workers in food-processing and manufacturing equipment operations. This area receives the greatest training emphasis because it involves the largest group of employees and has the greatest potential impact on product quality and overall productivity. Both target groups receive training in equipment setup, operation, and maintenance (as well as safety and hazard communication) from the training staff located at their assigned plant. Training includes some classroom instruction, but the greatest emphasis is on on-the-job training to maximize hands-on experience with the equipment. Training is provided to technicians and craft workers when they are initially employed, when new equipment is installed or new procedures are implemented, and when actual performance varies from preestablished performance standards. To monitor equipment operations, Frito-Lay's senior and plant managers, with assistance from technical trainers, have established job performance standards for equipment operators. In each plant, a computer that interfaces with individual equipment gathers equipment operational and production data and compares them with the equipment operator's performance standards. The results are used by the plant's technical trainers to evaluate the effectiveness of existing training programs and to identify new training requirements. The plant trainers then convey this data to the central trainers who modify the courseware as necessary or develop new programs if required. This system enables the technical training staff to target remedial training more accurately toward specific deficiencies.

Although receiving less emphasis, technical training also supports the technicians and craft workers located at Frito-Lay's distribution and marketing facilities. Training at the distribution facilities primarily involves the operation (and safety) and maintenance of material-handling equipment. Training at the marketing facilities involves the maintenance of delivery vehicles. Training is usually provided upon initial employment and whenever new equipment is purchased or installed. Training is also provided to address specific operating or maintenance problems. Similar to training in the plants, the greatest emphasis is on hands-on training, although some classroom instruction is also used.

Linkages. Because technical training is considered so critical to Frito-Lay's success, it is conducted separately and therefore is not linked to other training.

Frito-Lay is currently experimenting with a variation of Japanese management known as "high performance systems." Under this program, all workers are receiving an orientation, presented by technical trainers, in food-processing and production standards. Following completion of this orientation program, workers will be empowered to correct any processes that do not meet the standards.

There is a reverse linkage between technical training and the human resource function. Technical training assists in developing job performance standards for equipment operators. These standards are then used as the basis for appraisal and compensation. The computer interface with production equipment provides the data to determine performance variations.

Training Support of Strategic Goals

At Frito-Lay, technical training is directly involved in the corporate strategic goal and planning development process. The company generally establishes its strategic goals from three to five years in advance. These goals include overall corporate direction as well as more specific manufacturing and production objectives and standards. During the actual planning and strategy session, a representative from central training provides input and feedback concerning the potential impact of the proposed objectives and standards on training and the work force. Central training obtains the feedback data through continual interaction with the site trainers. Once the strategic goals are approved and implemented, central training develops corresponding training goals and objectives, which provide the parameters for training.

Most of the training curricula developed by central training for the individual plants directly support a corporate strategic goal or production objective or standard. For example, current plant training is primarily focused on increasing equipment operator skills and knowledge levels to achieve the goal of increasing productivity and improving product quality. Current training also promotes safety, which helps reduce equipment downtime and time lost from the job. Training further supports the corporate strategy of introducing new product variations by providing employees with the skills necessary to operate the equipment that produces the product.

Merck Pharmaceutical Manufacturing/ Merck & Company, Inc.

Merck & Company, Inc., is an international, research-intensive health products company focusing on the discovery, development, manufacture, and sale of human and animal health and specialty chemicals.

Merck is structured into the following major divisions: Merck Pharmaceutical Manufacturing Division, Merck Sharp & Dohme Division, Merck Sharp & Dohme International Division, Merck Sharp & Dohme Chemical Manufacturing Division, Merck Sharp & Dohme AGVET Division, Merck Sharp & Dohme Research Laboratories Division, Calgon Vestal Laboratories Division, Calgon Water Management Division, and Kelco Division. The company also includes Hubbard Farms, Inc., and its two operating units, Spafas, Inc., and British United Turkey, Ltd.

During 1988, Merck continued its strong performance with sales of $5.9 billion (an increase of 17 percent over 1987 sales) and net income of $1.2 billion (an increase of 33 percent). Overall, the company has eighteen plants in the United States, twenty-nine plants in seventeen other countries, and sixteen research facilities, seven or which are located in the United States. Merck employs 32,000 people.

Merck contributed significantly to global health in 1988 with the increased acceptance of its wide range of existing pharmaceuticals and the introduction of several new discoveries. Significant sales gains were achieved by Vasotec, which is used to treat high blood pressure and congestive heart failure; Pepcid, which is used to manage peptic ulcers; Noroxin and Primaxin, which are anti-infection medications; and Recombixax HB, the first genetically engineered vaccine for hepatitis licensed for human use. In 1988, Merck also introduced Prinivil, a blood pressure product in the same medication class in which Vasotec is dominant.

In September 1987, Merck introduced Mevacor, a drug to reduce cholesterol levels. In its first twelve months on the U.S. market, it achieved higher sales than any other prescription medication ever achieved in a similar period. Merck also initiated its plan to distribute free to Third World countries Meotizan, a drug for the treatment of river blindness, a parasitic disease affecting people in certain impoverished tropical areas. The company chose to donate the drug in order to accelerate the treatment process rather than to market the product for profit.

Overall, in 1988, Merck had fifteen drugs for human health in nine therapeutic classes that achieved worldwide sales of $100 million. This was an increase from thirteen drugs in eight classes in 1987. Also in 1988, the company's highly successful animal health drug Ivermectin garnered $100 million in sales for the third consecutive year.

In addition to its highly successful products, Merck & Company's strong performance can be attributed to judicious asset management, productivity improvements through the implementation of new technologies, and continual monitoring of costs to ensure that they increase more slowly than corresponding revenues. Merck has ensured that all of its operations remain lean and competitive. Since the company also maintains significant operations outside the United States, the strengthening of foreign currencies relative to the dollar has also contributed to the company's strong performance.

To maintain its leadership in the pharmaceuticals industry, Merck has invested extensively in research and development. Approximately 3,600 people are involved in pharmaceutical chemical research in its facilities located throughout the world. In 1988, Merck allocated $669 million for research and development, up 15 percent from 1987 funding levels. In 1989, Merck planned to invest $755 million in research and development. Within the pharmaceutical industry, Merck's 1988 research spending represented more than 10 percent of the estimated total for the U.S. industry. Approximately 75 percent of Merck's research is carried out in the United States.

Due to the nature of its business, Merck depends heavily on the creativity and productivity of its employees for its continued success. As a result, the company strives to provide a work environment that encourages excellence and achievement. The company is also committed to continual training and development as a means of providing the skills and technical knowledge necessary for its employees to perform at the highest levels. Merck has developed a multiyear plan that includes providing its managers and supervisors with the skills they need to manage the work force effectively. Some of the topics covered in the plan include how to select the best people, how to coach, how to provide appropriate rewards for outstanding performance, and how to foster open, interactive communication among departments. A more advanced series of development programs has been designed for company executives. These programs include a number of advanced management seminars that are conducted both in the United States and at Oxford University in England.

Merck Pharmaceutical Manufacturing Division (MPMD) was established on January 1, 1989, to produce animal and human health products for Merck marketing divisions worldwide. Using active ingredients produced in bulk by the Merck Chemical Manufacturing Division, MPMD formulates and packages drugs in a variety of dosage forms, as well as the full range of Merck vaccines.

Comprised of 5,400 people and twenty-one manufacturing facilities in fourteen countries, MPM was formed by consolidating manufacturing activities that formerly operated separately in the United States, Canada, and elsewhere around the world.

Merck Sharp & Dohme Division, Merck's human pharmaceuticals division, is the largest marketer of prescription medication in the United States, providing more than 150 prescription pharmaceuticals and vaccines. It has fifteen regional sales offices and fifteen distribution branches in the United States.

Strategic Goals

Merck & Company's primary strategy is to provide patients, physicians, and society with innovative pharmaceutical and chemical products of superior value and representing the latest findings in human and animal medical research and agricultural disease treatment. Merck intends to capitalize on the significant potential of its existing product lines and on new products that will continue to flow from its research and development activities. The company's research operations will play a critical role, with new discoveries and developments, in compensating for sales losses from older drugs whose patents will expire. Merck also expects that within the next ten years, its research operations will discover and develop new products in entirely new therapy classes that will serve new categories of patients. In addition to sustaining growth through the expansion of existing product lines and the discovery of new products, Merck will intensify its efforts to obtain promising new products and discoveries developed outside the company through acquisition, licensing agreements, and joint ventures. Finally, the company intends to continue its campaign to reduce costs and to improve productivity through the implementation of new technologies.

Training Structure

Within Merck & Company, general "soft skills" training for all its divisions and functions is controlled centrally by Corporate Human Resources. The company's technical training efforts are somewhat more decentralized to the division level because the divisions are involved in different operations that have unique training requirements. In addition to the Corporate Technical Training Department, each division has its own technical training structure and program that responds to the needs of that division's operations. The technical training function discussed in this case study is limited to the Merck Pharmaceutical Manufacturing division.

Organization. Within Merck Pharmaceutical Manufacturing, technical training is generally designed and developed centrally but delivered decentrally. Technical training has two subfunctions: Good Manufacturing Practices and an apprenticeship program. Good Manufacturing Practices are detailed procedures concerning the manufacture, processing, packaging, and distribution of drug products. They are mandated by company policies and U.S. Food and Drug Administration regulations. Technical training directly supports Good Manufacturing Practices by providing the requisite skills required for employees to perform under each of the four functions. The division's apprenticeship program involves extensive on-the-job training in the areas of operations and maintenance.

Because the requirements for quality products and for skilled employees are so critical, line managers play a very active role in technical training. Department managers actually have the responsibility for ensuring that each employee assigned to their department is properly trained in both specific job skills and in Good Manufacturing Practices required for the particular job. Each manager continually monitors the performance of all department employees and, with the assistance of the technical training staff, determines whether additional training is required. To assist with this evaluation, line mangers also review discrepancy reports generated by quality control experts and also continually monitor the manufacturing, processing, and packaging operations.

Although most training is presented decentrally by either the technical training staff or certified trainers, line managers also assume some responsibility for actual training delivery. Managers most frequently present safety training, which is tailored to accommodate their department's specific function and equipment. Moreover, line managers may elect to present some skill-building training through either coaching or other on-the-job training.

Staffing. Merck's corporate technical training staff consists of one training manager and five staff members for the Good Manufacturing Practices technical skills training area and four staff members in the apprenticeship training area. A representative of the technical training staff (usually a subject matter expert) is also located at each of three satellite plants (in Virginia, North Carolina, and Puerto Rico) to coordinate training. Staff members are selected for their technical expertise and their training potential. Prior to actual involvement in the training process, each new staff member is enrolled in extensive training that consists of the following: train-the-trainer programs, conducted by the American Management Association; competency-based training design, development, and evaluation, presented by Educational Systems of the Future; and Good Manufacturing Practices overview, provided by the Center for Professional Advancement. Following completion of the programs, each attendee receives a formal evaluation and critique of his or her newly acquired skills and knowledge based on criterion-referenced training standards. If a participant does not meet the standards, he or she may repeat the programs. All trainers also receive an average of two weeks of skill update training annually.

The Merck Pharmaceutical Manufacturing Division's staff can also request assistance from the Merck Corporate Technical Skills Training Group. This group, which is located at the headquarters facility, is available upon request to all divisions to provide specialized technical training expertise to address specific problems. It also has resources to assist in developing training needs analyses and courses. In addition, the training staff can borrow personnel from other training areas (including nontechnical training functions) on an as-needed basis under a companywide training staff sharing system. This system allows each training function within the company to develop specialized training expertise and share that expertise with others throughout the organization, thereby reducing costly duplication of effort.

Outside training consultants are also used on occasion to assist in conducting training needs analysis and to design and develop courses. Almost all training delivery, however, is accomplished by the technical training staff of certified trainers within the division. Approximately 10 percent of the training effort is contracted out.

Generally, the Merck Pharmaceutical Manufacturing training staff conducts all needs analyses and designs and develops training centrally for each of the division's plants. Training presentation, however, is usually accomplished on-site at the plants (to minimize work disruption) by the central staff, a certified trainer, or the on-site plant training representative. On occasion, the plant training representative may actually become involved with design and development in response to a training need unique to that plant.

Target Groups. Technical training at Merck's facilities primarily involves training technicians and craft workers engaged in manufacturing and packaging operations and in equipment maintenance. Although there is an occasional training effort involving technical professionals, most of their training is accomplished under a different training area. All management employees receive training conducted by the corporate human resource function. There are approximately 2,500 technical employees within the four Merck plants in the United States.

The focal point of all operational and some maintenance technical training is Good Manufacturing Practices, which includes pharmaceutical production and control, packaging and labeling, and storage and distribution. Training is targeted toward both update training and deficiency training. Update training in both manufacturing and packaging is modulated by company policy and U.S. Food and Drug Administration regulation and includes a review of all operational procedures. Deficiency training covers specific problem areas isolated by quality control inspections. Workers also receive training whenever new equipment or procedures are implemented or when they are transferred to a new position (for example, from a capsule packaging line to a compressing process). On average, each employee receives a minimum of two days of technical training per year and two days of personal development instruction per year.

Although regulated by the U.S. Food and Drug Administration, most of the maintenance technical training is procedural, involving actual equipment maintenance performance. Aside from training mandated by the Good Manufacturing Practices, most training is either refresher, delivered when problems are identified, or initial, delivered when new equipment is installed.

The apprenticeship program is primarily for new employees involved in operations or maintenance. It includes off-site and on-site classroom instruction and on-the-job training for several job areas within manufacturing and packaging or equipment maintenance. The apprentice actually rotates through several of the manufacturing and packaging production lines.

Training techniques and media vary widely, depending on specific needs, and include classroom training, individual self-paced instruction, computer-assisted training with interactive videodisc, and on-the-job training.

Linkages. There are three areas of linkage between technical and other types of training. First, safety training is combined with technical training when an employee is training in the operation of equipment or in manufacturing processes. Safety reinforcement training and periodic mandated training, such as hearing conservation, are provided separately by the respective department managers. Second, there is a link with other training through the training staff sharing system. In this system, training expertise is transferred among the different training functions. Finally, a less direct link exists between technical training and management/supervisory training. Because line managers are responsible for ensuring that their personnel have the required skills and training support to perform their jobs, Merck has developed the Supervisor Training Enhancement Program. In addition to the typical supervisory skills curriculum, the program also emphasizes the necessity for technical training in developing and maintaining a skilled work force that helps the company achieve its goals.

The main area of linkage between technical training and other human resource functions is with the apprenticeship program, in which apprentices must attain a specified skill level prior to promotion to journeyman status. Another link exists in the packaging operations area, in which workers receive bonuses for production exceeding the standard. Technical training increases both skills and productivity levels, thus enabling workers to achieve above-standard performance.

Training Support of Strategic Goals

Technical training supports Merck & Company's strategic goals by developing and maintaining a highly skilled and productive work force that produces high-quality products. Although not contributing directly to the company's primary goal of discovering and developing new products, the production of quality pharmaceutical products is of paramount concern to the company in maintaining its preeminence in the industry. Furthermore, a skilled and productive work force assists in reducing production costs. The total commitment to training by Merck & Company has been established in corporate policies and is fully supported by all of management from Chairman P. Roy Vagelos and top managers to first-line supervisors.

Motorola

Motorola, Inc., is one of the world's leading manufacturers of electronic equipment, components, and systems serving the U.S. and international markets. It is a leader in the production of cellular telephones, two-way mobile radios, pagers, and modems. The company is one of the few end-equipment manufacturers that also has extensive expertise in semiconductor technology and government electronics. In 1987, Motorola increased its sales by 12 percent, to $6.7 billion, and its net income by 62 percent, to $308 million. The company employs 97,700 people in plants and distribution and sales facilities located throughout the world.

Motorola is organized into seven major business sectors that, in turn, consist of approximately fifty groups and divisions. The following paragraphs summarize the products and major markets of each business sector.

The Communications Group designs and manufactures two-way radios, pagers, and other electronic communication systems. Its market areas include the construction, transportation, telephone, mining, petroleum, health care, electric utility, and agricultural industries. It also targets the educational sector and federal, state, and local governments.

The Semiconductor Products Group designs and produces a broad line of discrete semiconductors and integrated circuits that include microprocessors, microcomputers, and memory devices. Its products serve the advanced systems needs of the computer, automotive, consumer, industrial, telecommunications, and defense and other federal government markets.

The Information Systems Group provides all elements for distributed data systems, from basic modems to integrated network management systems. This group was formed to combine and integrate the capabilities of CODEX Corporation and Universal Data Systems, both previous Motorola acquisitions.

The Government Electronics Group specializes in research, development, and production of advanced electronics equipment and systems for the U.S. Department of Defense, the National Aeronautics and Space Administration, and other government agencies. The group also serves commercial users and international customers.

The General Systems Group designs and manufactures computer-based cellular radiotelephone systems, mobile and portable radiotelephones, microcomputer boards, and information-processing and -handling equipment for multiuser microcomputer systems.

The Automotive and Industrial Electronics Group develops and produces a variety of electronic modules, components, and power conversion equipment supporting the motor vehicle, industrial equipment, and major appliance industries.

Motorola's last group, New Enterprises, includes all activities engaged in completely new business areas. Most of these emerging growth, high-technology activities are in the areas of semiconductor equipment, hospital clinical information systems, factory automation, and real-time distributed computing systems.

Motorola's performance over the past ten years has been excellent, having achieved a 20 percent annual growth rate during each of those years. Its success has earned it the distinction of being the most continuously successful electronic product manufacturer in the United States. Founded in 1929 as a manufacturer and marketer of automobile radios, the company has become a producer of a variety of electronics products for the automobile, data-processing, communication, aerospace, and defense industries. Motorola attributes its success to the continuity and stability of its management and to its steadfast policy of diversifying only into related lines of business.

By not diversifying outside the electronics and electronics-related business areas, Motorola has remained in an industry that has become increasingly competitive. Both Japanese manufacturers and U.S. corporations that have expanded into electronics are increasing their presence in the industry. In fact, since 1982, three large Japanese corporations have become the leading worldwide manufacturers of semiconductor devices, surpassing both Motorola and Texas Instruments. Other Motorola products, from cellular telephones to computer modems, are also under increasingly competitive pressure.

To remain successful in the electronics industry, Motorola intends to rely heavily on its employees to provide its competitive edge. The company considers its people a renewable resource and has therefore developed a large training and education infrastructure to keep its work force abreast of the latest product and manufacturing technologies. In fact, when other major U.S. companies resorted to massive employee layoffs in response to increasing foreign competition, Motorola turned to training to update employee skills.

To benefit fully from its highly trained work force, Motorola has developed a participatory environment. The Participative Management Program encourages an informed and involved work force and a supportive and accessible management. All new employees receive training in the participative concept and are informed of their responsibility to contribute. All employees actually participate through work teams that are assigned production and profitability objectives. Each team then decides how best to achieve the objectives, and teams exceeding the objectives receive a profit share.

Strategic Goals

Motorola's overall goal is to become the best in its class in terms of technology, products, manufacturing, service, marketing, and people. To accomplish this broad goal, Motorola has established a number of objectives.

First, the company is pursuing a zero-defects program to improve product quality. Its goals are to achieve a tenfold increase in quality within two years and a hundredfold increase within four years. By 1992, Motorola intends to achieve *six sigma,* which is a statistical term translating into a 99.9997 percent quality perfection rate. The company also works closely with suppliers to ensure their compliance with strict quality control. In fact, suppliers are required to enroll in Motorola's quality control training courses.

Second, Motorola is seeking to reduce cycle times for product development and shipment. For new products, the company intends to reduce the time required to take a product from the concept stage through the design and manufacturing stages. Rapid product development is critical in the electronics industry because new technologies are being introduced constantly and rapidly. For existing products, the company intends to reduce the time it takes to deliver a product to the customer, from order placement and production to delivery.

Third, Motorola is continuing to improve its responsiveness to customers by accelerating delivery response times and by being more flexible in manufacturing specialized products. Because the company is itself a supplier of semiconductor devices, it recognizes the need to respond to its customers' needs for customized computer chips.

Fourth, Motorola is continuing its ongoing program to reduce costs. It has developed a just-in-time inventory system to help reduce the increasing costs of maintaining an inventory. The company also hopes to benefit from new, more efficient production methods that will be developed by its work teams. The teams have financial incentives to develop more productive techniques within their manufacturing areas.

Training Structure

Organization. Generally, training is centrally controlled, coordinated, and managed for subject matter that is applicable companywide and decentrally controlled and coordinated for subject matter that is specific to a plant or other facility. Centrally, all training is the responsibility of the Motorola Training and Education Center, while decentrally, it is the responsibility of the local training departments.

The Motorola Training and Education Center is an in-house employee training and education organization whose task is to improve individual and organizational performance and productivity on a worldwide corporate basis. Its operations include a central staff and facility located near Motorola's headquarters and five regional training centers, each with a staff and facility, located in Schaumburg, Illinois; Austin, Texas; Phoenix, Arizona; Geneva, Switzerland; and Kuala Lumpur, Malaipia. The centerpiece of the Motorola Training and Education

Center is the Galvin Center for Continuing Education (located in Schaumburg, Illinois), which is a state-of-the-art training facility with thirteen classrooms; a 180-seat auditorium; computer-aided design and manufacturing, robotics, and computer laboratories; advanced audiovisual systems; and satellite hookup capabilities. Small training facilities are located at several of the regional training centers and plants.

Created in 1980, the Motorola Training and Education Center has evolved into a multifaceted training service organization that supports the company by means of several activities and services. The center's primary mission is to design, develop, deliver, and evaluate training courses that apply throughout the company and that address the company's strategic goals. The courses are presented either in regularly scheduled sessions at most company training facilities or in special sessions at a time and location convenient to the trainee group. As mandated by its mission, all training provided by the center must support the company's current strategic goals. Its current courses address issues such as product quality, inventory reduction, and customer service. Training provided by the center is performance based and operates on a charge-back system. The center continually evaluates its courses, through feedback from the participants and their managers, and makes modifications as necessary.

The process of identifying the corporate strategic goals and the associated training requirements is a continuous effort involving high-level committee meetings. First, the Motorola Training and Education Center's advisory board, which is comprised of the company's senior executives (including Motorola's chairman), meets twice a year to chart the corporate strategic plan, determine general training direction, and develop a general budget for each of five broad functional areas. Second, the Motorola Training and Education Center's functional advisory councils (five councils representing engineering, manufacturing and materials, marketing, personnel, and sales) meet to translate the executive advisory board's training guidance into specific plans for each functional area. The advisory councils meet quarterly to identify and prioritize specific training requirements. Finally, the Motorola Training and Education Center's staff actually designs and develops courseware on the basis of the councils' guidelines. All courses are synopsized individually and within specific functional career paths in a comprehensive publication issued by the center.

A second mission of the center is to assist, upon request, the local training departments in designing, developing, delivering, and evaluating the unique training courses required for their specific facilities. Staff training members located at the center or regional training facilities can help identify training needs, develop a training curriculum, coordinate and implement the actual training course, and evaluate the course to measure training quality and effectiveness. The center can also either present the course on-site or train and assist the local trainers. Moreover, the center staff is available to assist local training departments in preparing a training strategy that addresses the future goals of the specific plant.

The third mission of the center is to provide special services and programs. Its special services include computer-based training in electronics concepts, terminology, and techniques; training for the company's suppliers in the areas of quality and just-in-time inventories; and satellite-delivered courses that provide professional training to many of Motorola's engineers and technical workers. Its special programs include the Computer-Aided Design and Manufacturing Conference; the Manufacturing Management Institute for Engineering, Manufacturing, and Operations Excellence; Foreign Study Tours; the Organizational Performance System; and the Senior Executive Program. The center also participates in the National Technological University–Satellite Delivery Program, which provides graduate-level courses for engineers needing state-of-the-art skills. All courses originate from major U.S. universities via satellite hookup and lead to degrees in the areas of computer engineering, computer sciences, electrical engineering, engineering management, and manufacturing systems engineering.

In addition to the Motorola Training and Education Center, there are local training departments that design, develop, and deliver specialized courses for specific plants. Motorola believes that these local training operations, which are closely associated with the plants, are best suited to identifying and supporting each plant's training requirements. The Motorola Training and Education Center is available to provide expertise, additional resources, or consultation.

Overall, Motorola allocates approximately $44 million a year to its training and education effort. This amount, which represents 2.4 percent of its payroll, is more than twice as much as the average company allocates.

Staffing. Motorola employs more than 800 trainers and supporting administrators at the Motorola Training and Education Center and in the local training departments. While a majority of the trainers at the center are professional trainers with some subject matter experience, additional subject matter experts represent each of Motorola's five functional areas. The center also uses several hundred freelance writers and contracted instructors to supplement its training development and delivery segments. In addition, the center relies on area community colleges, universities, and technical institutes for select training, both on- and off-site.

The local training departments employ more subject matter experts for their operations because the training involves specific manufacturing and processing techniques and procedures. These local training staffs are supplemented by the Motorola Training and Education Center staff (upon request) and by outside consultants. The center provides an extensive train-the-trainer program for new trainers and periodic refresher courses for existing trainers.

Target Groups. At Motorola, managers, engineers, technical professionals, and craft workers receive technical training. Managers and engineers receive the majority of their training through the Motorola Training and Education Center's special programs and seminars. Managers are primarily trained through classroom seminars and special programs that address current issues affecting the company's operations. The company's engineers, who receive more technically oriented training, are trained through classroom instruction, satellite courses, and computer-based training programs. Technical professionals and craft workers receive both general training, applicable companywide, and job-specific training, applicable to a particular plant. General training, which is technical, is presented to these target groups by the center via classroom instruction, computer-based programs, and to a lesser extent, satellite-delivered courses. The job-specific training is usually presented by the local training department at the individual plant and consists of classroom training, computer-based programs, and on-the-job training.

Training content is limited to subject matter that is job related and/or that supports the corporate strategic goals. Training provided by local facilities is exclusively job related and involves specific techniques, functions, procedures, and product lines. Training conducted by the center is general in nature and is more likely to support a corporate goal, such as zero defects/quality control, customer relations, and inventory control/material management. While the center's training courses can be technical, they always assume a companywide perspective, regardless of the subject matter. (The Motorola Training and Education Center believes that specific subject matter training is more appropriate for the local training functions.)

While the local training departments develop and provide training for specific needs, the Motorola Training and Education Center currently offers seventy-eight courses and 111 films that encompass six major career development tracks. A recent course catalog issued by the center lists the courses and films and provides training approaches and plans for each of the following tracks: creativity and benchmarking, engineering, inventory management, manufacturing operations, sales, and statistical process control. In addition to these career tracks, the center also offers courses concerning the participative environment.

Linkages. Because the Motorola Training and Education Center is responsible for a majority of the companywide training, most of the training is interrelated. The center offers a variety of courses representing functional areas such as management development, sales, personnel management, interpersonal skills, organization development, negotiation, and foreign languages. These lower-technology skills may be presented individually or combined with higher-technology skills under a multidisciplinary curriculum. As an example, the manufacturing operations management development career path includes courses in effective meetings and interpersonal skills as well as in applied diagnostic tools, work-in-progress/cycle time, and statistical process control.

Training is also linked to Motorola's participative management program. First, upon initial employment, each manager and employee receives orientation in participative management and what to expect in a participative environment. Second, the program encourages all employees to continually update their skills through the company's training programs in order to maximize their contribution to their assigned work teams. In fact, training is frequently used as a tool for each team to increase its productivity and efficiency and exceed its respective production and profitability objectives.

Technical training is also linked to the employee appraisal system through the company's Annual Performance and Career Plan. With this plan, the employee and supervisor review the employee's preceding year performance and determine whether the employee has met his or her career development goals. On the basis of this review, the employee and supervisor jointly determine whether further training and education are necessary.

Training Support of Strategic Goals

All training at Motorola directly supports the company's strategic goals. Through meetings of the Motorola Training and Education Center's executive advisory board and functional advisory councils, training is targeted to specific company issues and corporate objectives. The center continually evaluates the effectiveness of all training in terms of how it supports the company's strategic goals and updates the courses as necessary.

Training supports Motorola's basic philosophy that its employees are a renewable resource that should be trained for the mutual benefit of the company and the individual. Only through its well-trained and highly skilled work force can Motorola continue its successful performance in the increasingly competitive electronics industry.

Northern Telecom

Northern Telecom Inc. is a wholly owned U.S. subsidiary of Canadian-based Northern Telecom, Ltd., which is the world's leading manufacturer of fully digital telecommunications systems and major producer of office information management systems. Its products and related services are used by telephone companies, government and military agencies, and businesses and institutions throughout the world. Northern Telecom operates forty manufacturing plants, of which twenty-four are located in Canada, thirteen in the United States, two in Malaysia, and one in Ireland. The company has research and development operations in twenty-four of its forty manufacturing plants as well as in nine research facilities. Of these, three are located in Canada, five in the United States, and one in the United Kingdom. Northern Telecom employs a total of 48,778 people worldwide.

Northern Telecom manufactures a wide range of telecommunications equipment within five major product areas. The first area is central office switching systems, which are used by telephone companies to interconnect their customers' lines. Since the mid-1970s when Northern Telecom introduced its fully digital DMS central office switches, the company has remained the leading producer of the switches, with the largest worldwide installed base of fully digital switches. The second product area is voice and data transmission systems, which include fiber optical, microwave, and satellite communications equipment. Northern Telecom is currently developing and testing a fiber optical and switching network in a Florida community. The network will deliver integrated voice, data, and video services over one line. The third area is data connectivity equipment and related software, which enable the transmission of data through complex communications systems with greater speed, quality, and reliability. The fourth area is private branch exchanges, which are business communications systems located at customers' facilities and control voice and data communications among telephone terminals. The company leads this product area with the Meridian SL-1 system, which is the most widely used, fully digital system in the world. Northern Telecom's fifth product area is telephone terminals, which include residential, business, and public telephone sets, hands-free units, automatic dialers, business workstations, and integrated voice/data terminals.

During 1987, Northern Telecom, Ltd., earned $328.8 million in net income (an increase of 14.7 percent) on revenues of $4.85 billion (an increase of 10.7 percent). This record financial performance is largely attributed to the continued success of existing products that incorporate state-of-the-art technologies and excellent quality and reliability. The success also reflects the company's complete dedication to its customers by providing products with the greatest value and flexibility to meet their needs.

Northern Telecom's success during 1987 can also be attributed to new product and technology advances and to continued market expansion. During that year, Northern Telecom introduced numerous types of equipment and applications that advanced the Integrated Services Digital Network. Promoted by the company, the network creates international technical standards that permit the networking of voice, data, and images through international telecommunications systems. Northern Telecom also introduced the highly advanced DMS SuperNode digital switch system, which provides twice the processing power of previous DMS switches (this will increase to five times the previous processing power by 1990), thereby enabling telephone companies to provide more sophisticated new services to their customers. The Meridian Customer Defined Networking System, which provides greatly enhanced power, control, and flexibility over public and private telecommunications networks, was also introduced during 1987. This system enables large corporate, medical, and education customers to better control and modify the telecommunications systems located on their premises. Among a number of major sales overseas during 1987, the company successfully marketed its Packet Switching Network System to the West German government for use in the new national air traffic control communications network.

Northern Telecom also concentrated on market expansion during 1987. The company intensified its efforts in its primary North American market by targeting key regions in which deregulation and growth have created potential opportunity. The company also pursued selective expansion within its newer markets in Europe and the United Kingdom, Africa, the Near East, the Indian subcontinent, Japan, and the Pacific Rim. As a result, Northern Telecom penetrated new markets in Japan, West Germany, New Zealand, Australia, France, and the United Kingdom. Future expansion may include joint ventures with leading manufacturers of a targeted region or, if appropriate, acquisition.

Northern Telecom's extensive research and development operations have also contributed to its success by developing increasingly more innovative communications systems and equipment with state-of-the-art technologies that meet customers' needs. During 1987, Northern Telecom increased its research spending by 12 percent to $588 million. Over the next five years the company will double the $2.1 billion that was allocated for research and development between 1982 and 1987. The company recognizes that only through extensive research can it remain a leader in the highly competitive and rapidly growing telecommunications industry.

Northern Telecom projects that future growth of the telecommunications industry will be explosive and unmatched by any other industry, reaching $300 billion in revenues from the current $75 billion by the year 2000. The trend toward global economics and the development of new technologies and new generations of information management equipment are expected to increase the need for more sophisticated and efficient telecommunications networks and systems with greater capacity. Additionally, Northern Telecom believes that a sophisticated global telecommunications system is the most effective means of increasing productivity and international competitiveness because of its ability to network a wide range of voice, data, and video communications systems. As a result, the company believes that most developing and developed governments will be expanding, modernizing, or replacing their present telecommunications systems.

Northern Telecom intends to capitalize on that growth and remain a leader by focusing on the five major product areas that it envisions as central to the telecommunication industry's future growth. Within the central office switching product area, total annual revenue in just the North American market is expected to increase from the current $6 billion to more than $12 billion by the year 2000. This growth will result from new demands by business customers for services that are now available through new high-technology switches such as the DMS Super-Node. To maximize its growth potential in switch products, Northern Telecom will continue designing its products to permit upgrading as new technologies evolve. The transmission equipment product area is expected to grow from $4 billion in annual revenue to $20 billion by the year 2000. Demand by business users and telephone companies for the greater capacity and flexibility afforded by optical fiber and microwave transmission equipment will lead the growth. The data connectivity product area will be the fastest-growing area in the North American market, with an anticipated growth in annual revenue from the current $3 billion to more than $20 billion by the year 2000. Northern Telecom intends to lead the growth with state-of-the-art products such as the LANSTAR data system, which provides an interface among equipment from different manufacturers. The private business exchange product area is expected to increase in just North America from $4 billion in annual revenue to $15 billion by the year 2000. Demands for new enhanced services, such as voice and text messaging and call accounting, and deregulation of several key markets will provide the growth opportunity within this product area. Finally, the terminal product area is projected to grow from $4 billion in annual revenue to more than $15 billion by the year 2000. Demand for more sophisticated telephone terminals, such as intelligent pay phones and telephones with touch sensitive displays, will stimulate the growth.

Strategic Goals

Northern Telecom is pursuing the immediate strategic goal of strengthening its role as the leading manufacturer of fully digital telecommunications equipment. At the same time, the company is positioning itself for the long-term goal of becoming the worldwide leading producer of telecommunications equipment within a vastly expanded and highly competitive industry. To help the company concentrate its efforts on specific industry growth areas anticipated for the year 2000, Northern Telecom has established its "Vision 2000" plan. As currently reflected in the plan, the company believes that its five major product areas will have the greatest growth potential in the telecommunications industry.

To capitalize on that potential, Northern Telecom intends to continue designing and developing telecommunications products within the five highest potential growth areas that incorporate the latest innovations and technologies together with the highest degree of product quality and reliability. To support new product development and remain in the forefront of technical innovation, the company plans to continue its extensive research and development efforts. In fact, Northern Telecom is striving for technological advances that could establish industry standards for both products and performance. The company also intends to continue its aggressive expansion into new North American market segments as well as into new markets overseas. To support this expansion, the company will continue to position itself as a multinational producer and marketer of telecommunications equipment. The company will also continue its commitment to customer service by providing products with maximized value and flexibility to satisfy its customers' needs.

Northern Telecom will also continue to streamline its manufacturing operations to improve productivity and decrease operating costs through investments in new equipment and technologies. Additionally, the company will continue to encourage employee participation through the establishment of teams within select product development and manufacturing operations.

Training Structure

Organization. With the exception of management and professional development and sales and marketing training, which are normally designed, developed, and delivered centrally by Northern Telecom Inc.'s headquarters training operation, training, including technical training, is decentralized to division and plant levels. The central training operation, however, is responsible for designing and developing generic orientation and core technical training courseware for delivery by the product divisions to their technical and skilled workers. Decentralized training is considered the most effective system because many of the company's plants have unique and complex products and manufacturing operations. Northern Telecom therefore believes that its plants are best equipped with the operational expertise necessary to identify their own training requirements. The company also believes that by decentralizing training, the plants can respond more quickly with new and specific training programs to support the continual advancement of products and manufacturing technologies.

Being decentralized, technical training is conducted by training operations that join part of the two major operating divisions, Integrated Network Systems and Meridian Digital Services, and also by the individual plants when specialized or manufacturing procedures are involved. There is no formal organizational relationship and only minimal informal interface among the training operations because of their unique training requirements.

Because of the company's decentralized training structure, the rest of this case study is limited to a review of the technical training operations of the Integrated Network Systems Group and of the specialized semiconductor plant in Rancho Bernardo, California. The Integrated Network Systems Division is considered representative of divisional training operations, while the semiconductor plant provides an example of technical training's major role in supporting the plant's recent restructuring into work teams.

Within the Integrated Network Systems Group, which produces telecommunications switching and related equipment, technical training is generally designed and developed centrally at the group level and presented decentrally at the plant level. Training is basically organized under four activities: technical, which trains circuit- and system-level technicians and engineers; operations, which trains just-in-time inventory control and production; manufacturing, which trains product assemblers; and sales and marketing, which provides sales training to support specific switching products. The four training activities have no formal organizational linkages.

The Integrated Network Systems Group central training staff is responsible for designing and developing the training courseware. Because training is ultimately the responsibility and prerogative of division and plant operations managers, central training staff members serve as training consultants and facilitators in developing training programs that address specific operating problems or that support newly installed equipment. The central training staff works closely with both operations subject matter experts and operations staff trainers during the needs analysis and design and development phases to obtain the necessary technical expertise. The central training staff also provides train-the-trainer instruction and certification to the operations staff, which will actually conduct the training programs. The central training staff further assists operations staff trainers and managers in evaluating the effectiveness of training programs. Finally, the central staff may provide, upon request, assistance to the operations staff trainers during the actual training presentation.

Delivery of technical training within the division is the responsibility of operations personnel with subject matter expertise who have received instructor training and certification. Depending on the product or equipment, technical training is conducted either at the plants or at the division's central training facility in Raleigh, North Carolina, which offers equipment simulators as well as classrooms. Operations staff trainers are assigned to the central facility and the individual plants and report to operations management within those activities. Generally, manufacturing and operations training is accomplished at the specific plants, while circuit- and system-level training is accomplished on the equipment simulators at the central training facility.

Northern Telecom's semiconductor plant in Rancho Bernardo, California, manufactures application-specific integrated circuit components for use in Northern Telecom products. The plant has the primary advantage of being a secure and fully dedicated supplier that is being completely oriented toward Northern Telecom's products and manufacturing procedures and technologies. The plant is unique in that it does not report to any of Northern Telecom's major product divisions.

Following a 1984 audit that identified weaknesses in productivity and product quality, the plant's directors and top management accomplished a major restructuring designed to help achieve excellence and restore competitiveness. Prior to the restructuring, the plant's top managers established the objectives of making the plant the premier producer of semiconductors that can exploit all technological advances of the industry. The managers decided that to achieve that objective, the plant had to have an outward orientation to best capitalize on opportunities in the industry, a work force with advanced skills and knowledge, and improved communications and interface among plant functions.

As a result of the top-level planning, the Rancho Bernardo plant has been restructured to encourage employee participation, responsibility, and open communication. To support this new structure, several layers of management have been removed and plant functions such as manufacturing, finance, human resources, and technical training have been integrated into business "councils." One business council has been created for each of the plant's main activities, or "business units" (fabrication, testing, and assembly), to provide direction and suggestions and to allocate resources. Beneath each of the three business councils are three to twelve independent work teams, each of which is comprised of engineers, equipment technicians, ten to twelve operators, and a team manager. Each team has the authority to mobilize the resources necessary to accomplish any task, goal, or objective.

Technical training has been restructured to better support the plant's new work team organization. From the beginning, top managers have considered technical training absolutely critical to the success of the work teams. All work team operators and technicians have to be familiar with a variety of equipment and procedures to provide the versatility to operate, trouble-

shoot, and maintain each piece of equipment in a team's workstation. In addition, each work team member has to keep pace with
the rapidly changing product and manufacturing technologies
that continue to advance the semiconductor industry. To support these objectives, technical training has been included as
one of the functional responsibilities of the work teams. The work
teams are responsible for identifying and analyzing their training requirements, structuring a training program, and actually
conducting the training.

A technical training group has been established within
each of three business units. The technical training departments
within the business units serve as a consultant to the work teams
within each business unit. Each department's primary role is
to instruct each team in how to develop and conduct training
programs, to provide training materials as required, and to
evaluate the effectiveness of the work team's technical training.
The technical training department also functions as a research
unit for new training technologies and thus keeps abreast of the
latest training methods and how other companies within the industry conduct their training.

A training and education function, as part of the Human
Resources Department provides courses in both technical and
nontechnical subjects of interest to employees throughout the
division. The division's library is a part of this training and
education group and provides divisionwide course scheduling,
registration, and coordination. In addition, learning packages
on both technical and nontechnical subjects are available in audio
and video programs, interactive video, self-paced printed materials, and other forms.

Staffing. Of Northern Telecom's 900 technical trainers,
approximately 400 are involved in Integrated Network Systems
Group's technical, operations, manufacturing, and sales and
marketing training activities. Major programs are also available
to provide product operations and maintenance training to the
division's customers.

In each of the division's four training activities, a central
training staff accomplishes the needs analysis, designs and
develops the training courseware, and conducts instructor train-

ing for the training providers. The staff is comprised of human resource specialists who have backgrounds in adult education and instructional systems and subject matter experts who have had some exposure to adult education. Interestingly, once the subject matter experts transfer from operations to training, they lose their expert status and must rely on operations personnel for course data. This is intended to align training more closely with plant operating activities. The major consideration in selecting trainers is that candidates not be "dead ended" in the training function because training is considered a step in the career track rather than a career in itself. Each trainer must be capable of moving to other positions within the division or the corporation.

Generally, the central training staff approaches all training design and development operations as a team. A subject matter expert, who is the training "prime designate," is responsible for overall course content and as a result works closely with the operations personnel who have requested the training. A human resource specialist with an adult education background is responsible for organizing the content in the most effective manner for maximizing adult learning. Finally, a media specialist assists in developing the accompanying training material.

Training delivery is generally decentralized and the responsibility of operations staff members who have received instructor training. The operations training staff conducts training at the division's central training facilities and at the individual plants. The division's central training facilities are generally used to provide equipment simulation training to circuit- and system-level technical employees and equipment familiarization training to sales and marketing personnel. Manufacturing and operations training is accomplished at the plants to maximize actual hands-on instruction. The operations staff members also work with the operations personnel and the central training staff to help evaluate training effectiveness and to solve training problems.

Integrated Network Systems Group's customer service training is conducted separately from the other four training activities. The training is oriented more toward product operations and maintenance and is conducted by Customer Service

Department training staff members who are closely associated with the division. Customer service training is conducted in two major training centers at Research Triangle Park, North Carolina, and Sacramento, California.

The division uses contract providers for some technical training, primarily in the area of advanced technical training for engineers. Select community colleges and area universities are also used for technician and engineer career development. Moreover, original equipment manufacturers conduct some operations and maintenance training for skilled workers and technicians when new manufacturing equipment is installed.

Technical training at the Rancho Bernardo plant is primarily conducted by a training staff assigned to the technical training department within each of the three manufacturing business units and designated technical trainers within each work team. The technical training departments are comprised of specialists who have backgrounds in a variety of fields (mostly in integrated circuit manufacturing) and extensive training and education in instructional systems design and training methods. Their responsibilities include training each work team to become a self-training resource, assisting the teams in solving problems, providing the training materials necessary for the teams to conduct self-training, and evaluating the effectiveness of work team training. In addition, the training and education function within the Human Resources Department offers internal seminars, conducted by both internal and external trainers to acquaint engineers, technicians, and operators with new developing technologies and methods.

Under the new plant structure, each work team is responsible for identifying its technical training requirements, structuring a training program, and conducting the training. Depending upon the work team, responsibilities for technical training within the team may be assumed by the entire team, assigned to the team member best qualified in a specific area, or rotated among the members. In situations involving complex procedures or theories, the team engineer or technician may conduct the training; equipment operations and maintenance training is usually conducted by a team equipment operator. Generally, however, the team works as a unit to address operating problems and to develop potential training solutions.

Technical training at the plant is also provided by outside services through the plantwide training and education function. Through a satellite system offered by a local university, engineering and advanced engineering courses are provided to the plant's technicians and engineers. Technical schools and community colleges also offer courses to enhance skills and theoretical understanding for equipment operators and technicians. Finally, equipment manufacturers usually provide maintenance training for technicians in conjunction with the installation of new equipment. Training is sometimes also provided to operators of the newly installed equipment.

Target Groups. Technical training within the Integrated Network Systems Group varies widely since it is the sole responsibility and prerogative of the division and individual plant managers. Most managers see training as critical to their operations, and all new supervisors receive a training orientation that stresses the need for training. Most importantly, Northern Telecom has expressed its commitment to training as a major factor in its expansion efforts. Generally, all plants conduct some training, typically an orientation for new hires, remedial training to address specific deficiencies, update training to maintain manufacturing efficiency and productivity, and new equipment training. Training content covers manufacturing equipment operations and maintenance, circuit- and system-level testing, product assembly, and theory (for senior personnel). Overall, skilled workers and technicians receive the most training, which consists of training in equipment operations and maintenance and product testing. Engineers receive less training, which consists primarily of advanced engineering and theory training. Frequency of training also depends on the operations managers, who are responsible for developing their own employees. Most managers use a career development track to identify suggested courses to be taken by each employee at career milestones. An individual development plan is designed for each employee in order to identify strengths and weaknesses, recommend a career path, and develop a supporting training program. Annual evaluations are used to monitor the employee's progress and indicate whether additional training is required.

Depending on the target group and subject matter, technical training is conducted at the individual plants, at the division's central training facility, or at a noncompany off-site facility. The training media include classroom instruction, equipment simulation, computer-based training, satellite-transmitted courseware, self-paced training manuals, self-paced interactive video, and on-the-job training. All training courseware is continually evaluated by means of posttraining interviews and questionnaires to ensure maximum effectiveness.

The primary focus of technical training at the Rancho Bernardo plant is the work teams and their members—the engineer, the equipment technician, and the operators. Training involves subject matter relating to the three major activities of the plant: fabrication, testing, and assembly. Typically, operator training is conducted by the designated work team trainer either on-site at the workstation or in plant classrooms. Engineer and technician training is more likely to be conducted in the plant classroom by outside trainers and educators or by members of the technical training department.

To capitalize fully on the work team structure, each team member must have a breadth and depth of skills and knowledge to perform a multitude of tasks at more than one workstation. To help promote and monitor each member's development, the plant is in the process of establishing a knowledge and skill progression system. The system will provide four levels of certification—based on knowledge and experience—for each of the work team's workstations. Each member will be encouraged by the team to achieve top certification in all of its workstations. The plant's various technical training activities will play a major role in helping each member attain certification.

Linkages. Because the responsibility for technical training at both Integrated Network Systems and the semiconductor plant at Rancho Bernardo has been placed at the operations work level, there are no direct linkages with other training.

However, because of the complex nature of the division's switch products and the close proximity of the two training facilities, there is an indirect link between technical training and customer service training. Furthermore, because the company's management development and orientation training includes instruction in the use of technical training to achieve the corporate goals, there is an indirect link between management and technical training.

The closest link between the human resource function and technical training occurs within the Rancho Bernardo semiconductor plant. With its new structure, representatives from the technical training, human resource, manufacturing, production, and finance functions serve together to provide integrated direction, guidance, and resources to the work teams. Moreover, the divisionwide training and education function is a component within the Human Resources Department. The training and education function provides technical training courses of interest to employees throughout the division. This function also provides in-house training and education on instructional design and training skills to members of the technical training departments and to team trainers.

At the Integrated Network Systems Division, there is an indirect link between the human resource function and technical training because the division's central technical training staff reports through the human resource function.

Training Support of Strategic Goals

Technical training directly supports Northern Telecom's corporate strategy of becoming the world's leading producer of telecommunications equipment by the year 2000. Training will provide the advanced skills and knowledge necessary to excel in an industry that will be highly technical and fiercely competitive. It will provide the company's work force with the knowledge, skills, and understanding necessary to anticipate and correct potential production problems quickly and to recommend production and product improvements. It will also provide the depth and breadth of skills necessary for employees to become versatile members of work teams. Only through a completely involved and highly skilled work force can Northern Telecom produce highly advanced and reliable products that provide quality and value to the customer.

Northern Telecom's top managers recognize the absolute necessity of technical training in achieving the Vision 2000 strategic goal. Their commitment to training permeates all divisions of the company through all of the company's managers.

Appendix

Following is a listing of representative groups of occupations among technical professionals, technicians/technologists, and skilled trade workers.

I. Technical Professionals
    A.   Engineers, Architects, Surveyors
        1.   Engineers
                Aeronautical and Astronomical Engineers
                Ceramic Engineers
                Chemical Engineers
                Civil Engineers
                Electrical Engineers
                Industrial Engineers
                Material Engineers
                Mechanical Engineers
                Mine Safety Engineers
                Mining Engineers
                Metallurgical Engineers
                Nuclear Engineers
                Petroleum Engineers
        2.   Architects (excluding landscape and marine)
        3.   Surveyors
    B.   Natural, Computer, and Mathematical Science
        1.   Computer and Mathematical Occupations
                Actuaries
                Computer Systems Analysts
                Mathematicians

           Operations and Systems Researchers
           Statisticians
      2.   Life Scientists
           Agricultural Scientists
           Biological Scientists
           Foresters/Conservation Scientists
      3.   Physical Scientists
           Astronomers
           Chemists
           Geologists
           Geophysicists
           Meteorologists
           Oceanographers
           Physicists
C.   Health Diagnosing and Treating Occupations
      Audiologists
      Chiropractors
      Dentists
      Dieticians and Nutritionists
      Occupational Therapists
      Optometrists
      Pharmacists
      Physical Therapists
      Physicians and Surgeons
      Recreational Therapists
      Registered Nurses
      Respiratory Therapists
      Speech Pathologists
      Veterinarians and Veterinary Inspectors
D.   Transportation Occupations
      Aircraft Pilots
      Flight Engineers
      Ship Captains
II.   Technicians/Technologists
A.   Health Technicians and Technologists
      Clinical Lab Technicians and Technologists
      Dental Hygienists
      Dietetic Technicians

Electrocardiographic Technicians
Electroencephalograph Technicians
Emergency Medical Technicians
Licensed Practical Nurses
Medical and Clinical Lab Technicians/Technologists
Medical Records Technicians
Opticians, Dispensing and Measuring
Physician Assistants
Radiological Technicians and Technologists
Surgical Technicians

B. Engineering and Science Technicians and Technologists
Civil Engineering Technicians
Drafters
Electrical and Electronic Technicians/Technologists
Engineering Technicians
Industrial Engineering Technicians
Mechanical Engineering Technicians
Physical and Life Science and Math Technicians

C. Other Technologists and Technicians
Air Traffic Controllers
Broadcast Technicians
Computer Programmers
Photographers

D. Mechanics, Installers, and Repairers
Aircraft Mechanics and Engine Specialists
Automotive Body and Related Repairers
Automotive and Motorcycle Mechanics
Bicycle Repairers
Bus and Truck Mechanics
Coin and Vending Machine Servicers and Repairers
Communications Equipment Mechanics
Data-Processing Equipment Repairers
Diesel Engine Mechanics
Electrical Installers
Electrical and Electronic Equipment Mechanics
Electronics Home Entertainment Equipment Repairers

Electronic Meter Repairers and Installers
Electronical Medical/Biomedical Equipment Repairers
Electronics Commercial Equipment Repairers
Farm Equipment Mechanics
Heating, Air-Conditioning, and Refrigeration Mechanics
Home Appliance and Power Tool Repairers
Industrial Machinery Mechanics
Maintenance Repairers
Marine Machinery Maintenance Mechanics
Millwrights
Mine Machinery Mechanics
Mobile Heavy Equipment Mechanics
Mobile Home Repairers
Musical Instrument Repairers and Tuners
Office Machine and Cash Register Servicers
Precision Instrument Repairers
Radio Mechanics
Rail Car Repairers
Small Engine Mechanics
Telephone and Cable TV Installers and Repairers
Telephone Station Installers and Repairers
Textile Machine Maintenance Mechanics
Water and Power Plant Machinery and Mechanics

III.   Skilled Trade (Blue-Collar) Workers
    A.   Construction Workers
        Blasters
        Carpenters
        Electricians
        Pipefitters
        Plumbers
        Shipfitters
        Steamfitters
    B.   Precision Metal Workers
        Boilermakers
        Jewelers and Silversmiths
        Machinists

        Precision Graders
        Precision Inspectors
        Precision Testers
        Sheet Metal Workers
        Tool and Die Makers
        Watchmakers

C.   Plant and System Operators
        Chemical Plant and System Operators
        Petroleum Refinery and Control Plant Operators
        Stationary Engineers
        Water and Liquid Waste Treatment Plant Operators

References and Suggested Readings

Abram, R., Ashley, W., Faddis, C., and Wiant, A. *Preparing for High Technology: Programs That Work.* Columbus: National Center for Research in Vocational Education, Ohio State University, 1982.

American Federation of Labor–Congress of Industrial Organizations. *Policy Paper for 1988.* Washington, D.C.: American Federation of Labor—Congress of Industrial Organizations, 1988.

American Society for Training and Development. *Models of Excellence.* Alexandria, Va.: American Society for Training and Development, 1983.

Butler, R. "The Training of Skilled Trade Workers." Unpublished paper prepared for the American Society for Training and Development, Alexandria, Va., 1988.

Byrne, J. A. "The Rebel Shaking Up Exxon." *Business Week,* July 18, 1988, pp. 104–111.

Carey, M. L. *How Workers Get Their Training.* Bureau of Labor Statistics, Bulletin 2226. Washington, D.C.: U.S. Government Printing Office, March 1985.

Carnevale, A. P. *Human Capital: A High-Yield Corporate Investment.* Alexandria, Va.: American Society for Training and Development, 1983.

Carnevale, A. P. *Jobs For the Nation: Challenges for a Society Based on Work.* Alexandria, Va.: American Society for Training and Development, 1985.

Carnevale, A. P., and Gainer, L. J. *The Learning Enterprise.* Washington, D.C.: U.S. Government Printing Office, 1989.

Carnevale, A. P., Gainer, L. J., and Meltzer, A. S. *Workplace Basics: The Skills Employers Want.* Washington, D.C.: U.S. Government Printing Office, 1988.

Center for Educational Statistics. *Digest of Education Statistics 1987.* (T. Snyder, compiler.) Washington, D.C.: U.S. Government Printing Office, May 1987.

Choate, P. "Employability." In *Adult Learners and National Priorities: Emerging State and Federal Policies.* Proceedings of the National Invitational Conference on State and Federal Policy Affecting Adult Learners, Nov. 1985. Columbia, Md.: Commission on Higher Education and the Adult Learner, 1985.

Choulochas, J., and McKenney, K. "The Beat Goes On: Partnership Building." *Community, Technical, and Junior College Journal,* 1986, *56* (5), 62–64.

Cohen, S. L., L'Allier, J. J., and Stewart, D. "Interactive Videodisc—Then, Now, and Minutes from Now." *Training & Development Journal,* Oct. 1987, pp. 31–36.

Glover, R. W. *Apprenticeship in the United States: Implications for Vocational Education Research and Development.* Occasional Paper No. 66. Columbus: National Center of Research in Vocational Education, Ohio State University, 1986.

Goldstein, H. "Technical Workers in the United States." Unpublished paper developed for the American Society for Training and Development, Alexandria, Va., 1988.

Harwood, R. K. *Directions: A Guide to Career Planning.* Boston, Mass.: Houghton Mifflin, 1978.

Hull, D. M. "Preparing Technicians for Tomorrow's Jobs." In D. M. Hull (ed.), *Technician Education Directory.* (12th ed.) Ann Arbor, Mich.: Prakken, 1986.

Kimmerling, G. F. "The Youth Market: A Valuable Resource." *Training & Development Journal,* 1986, *40* (7), 59.

Lillard, L. A., and Tan, H. W. *Private Sector Training: Who Gets It and What Are Its Effects?* Report to the U.S. Department of Labor. Santa Monica, Calif.: Rand Corporation, 1986.

McDaniels, C. "Three of Many Possible Future Occupational Scenarios for the 1990s." *Journal of Cooperative Education,* 1986, *22* (2), 6.

National Academy of Engineering, Engineering Education and Practice in the United States. *Continuing Education of Engineers.* Washington, D.C.: National Academy Press, 1985.

National Research Council. *The Competitive Status of the United States Auto Industry.* Washington, D.C.: National Academy Press, 1982.

Smith, E. E., "Interactive Video: An Examination of Use and Effectiveness." *Journal of Instructional Development,* 1987, *10* (2), 2–10.

Stephan, E., Mills, G. E., Pace, R. W., and Ralphs, L. "HRD in the Fortune 500 — A Survey." *Training & Development Journal,* Jan. 1988, pp. 26–32.

"*Training* Magazine's Industry Report 1987." *Training,* Oct. 1987, pp. 33–72.

U.S. Department of Defense. *Military Manpower Training Report FY 1989.* Washington, D.C.: U.S. Department of Defense, 1988.

U.S. Department of Labor, Bureau of Labor Statistics. *Occupational Outlook Handbook.* Washington, D.C.: U.S. Government Printing Office, 1987.

U.S. Department of Labor, Bureau of Labor Statistics. *Occupational Projections and Training Data.* Washington, D.C.: U.S. Government Printing Office, 1986.

Warmbrod, C. P., Persavich, J.J., and L'Angelle, D. *Sharing Resources: Postsecondary Education and Industry Cooperation.* Columbus: National Center for Research in Vocational Education, Ohio State University, 1981.

West, E. "The Employer Map: The Organization of Technical Training." Unpublished paper developed for the American Society for Training and Development, Alexandria, Va., 1988.

William T. Grant Foundation Commission on Work, Family, and Citizenship. *The Forgotten Half: Noncollege Youth In America.* Washington, D.C.: The William T. Grant Foundation, 1988.

Work in America Institute. "Cost-Effective Design and Delivery of Training Programs." In *Training for New Technologies.* Scarsdale, N.Y.: Work in America Institute, 1987.

Index